CREATING THE RELATIONSHIP OF YOUR DREAMS

How to Manifest it from Fantasy to Reality

by Thomas E. Ziemann

Creating the Relationship of Your Dreams:
How to Manifest it From Fantasy to Reality

ISBN (paperback): 978-1-7347706-5-0
ISBN (ebook): 978-1-7347706-6-7

Library of Congress Cataloging-in-publication data Creating the
Relationship of Your Dreams: How to Manifest It From Fantasy to
Reality, Ziemann, Thomas LOCN: 2020914881

The Publishing Portal
Los Angeles, California
Printed in the United States of America

CREDITS

Author: Thomas E Ziemann
Editor/Contributor: Edie Weinstein www.opti-mystical.com
Co Contributor: Jennifer Blankl www.jenniferblankl.com
Foreword by Christian Conte' Ph.D. www.DrChristianConte.com
Publishing Manager Tisha Morris www.tishamorris.com
Creative Consultants: Lisa Peplow, Dorothy Cramer and Austin Vickers
Cover and Interior Designs: Eric Labacz www.labaczdesign.com
Photographer: Jessie Kirk www.jessiekirkphotography.com

CONTENTS

Part One:
Living, Loving and Learning About Relationships

Part Two:
Transform the Quality of Your Relationships

The following endorsements were provided by
Medical, Mental Health Professionals
and Clergy members:

Christian Conte- PhD

Bernie Siegel- MD

Gary Salyer- PhD

Steve McSwain- PhD

Shelley Leutschaf- PhD, LP

Cate Montana- MA

Terri Levine- PhD

Darian Flemming- LCSW, CRC

Rabbi Michael Shevack

Rev. Edie Weinstein- MSW, LSW

LOVING ENDORSEMENTS

"Many years ago I learned, as a doctor, the benefit of what Tom is teaching when a patient told me she needed to know how to live between office visits. Instead of focusing on their disease I started to help people heal their lives and find a life they loved. Our futures are unconsciously created long in advance. There are no coincidences. If you are wise enough to let Tom's book and wisdom coach and guide you the future and the relationship you create will be the one you desire. My wife and I, and our marriage, were perfect examples of the truth of his words. We loved each other and became like one person through our marriage and relationship."

—**Bernie Siegel, MD** author of *No Endings Only Beginnings and When You Realize How Perfect Everything Is*

"Finally, someone understands that to have the perfect Soulmate, one must make oneself the perfect Soulmate. Thomas teaches us the ancient truth that romance isn't the naïve dissolving of individuals inseparably into each other, but, quite the contrary, it requires real and respected boundaries. But, these boundaries, unlike ages past, are not cement. They are flexible; breathing, always open to the "seek-and-ye-shall-find" adventure of contemporary, spiritually-alive coupling.

Most critically, Thomas has put down, precisely, how to break the "rebound" cycle: where you break up someone, only to bring yourself the perfect reflection of your same psychological problem in a different body, only to break up again . . .

Ziemann has no Ph.D., C.S.W., no, M.D. But, he is far more qualified: he has made every mistake in the book, so he can actually write the book. He knows his stuff, because he has suffered to learn it. If you want to create the relationship of your dreams, Thomas Ziemann may be the man of your dreams."
—**Rabbi Michael Shevack**, Founder of "The Alliance for Enlightened Judaism". Author of six books, his latest, *Soul Lessons from the Wizard of Oz.*

"Tom Ziemann has done it again. In his first book he invited me into **The Department of Zenitation**. I followed him through his personal journey to self-awareness. As he decluttered his mind he showed me that I am the most important person in my life. I saw that the calmer and more satisfied with myself I was, the more I could be not just to other people, but the World itself. I took it as an Environmental Handbook of sorts that started within my heart and mind and expanded outward from there.

Next, he again got personal. I got a glimpse into his life, and, like mine, it always hasn't been wine and roses. In his second book **Taming the Anger Dragon: From Pissed Off to Peaceful**, he showed me that I am not alone in the day-to-day things that irritate, as well as those long-buried episodes in my life that have kept me two seconds away from explosive rage at times. Let's just say after careful consideration of what he shared my "fuse" is significantly longer and heaven knows I needed that. Now, that he'd passed on some really good suggestions for getting myself pointed in the right direction. I got to see how he has applied what he has learned in his journey of self-discovery and enlightenment.

I've just finished **Creating the Relationship of Your Dreams**. Therein was a roadmap in which he very thoughtfully laid out ideas for a person's journey through life that includes someone with whom you want to share your Heart, your Mind, and your Soul. Here he tells me "You know, learning from your own mistakes is fine, but learning from someone else's is easier." Tom has finally found some peace with a loving partner. They both are dedicated to what they need to do on a daily basis to make their home is a loving, happy place they hate to leave and always want to come back to. He showed me that a relationship should and could be a sanctuary... a place where being yourself... letting yourself live and love in peace is not really difficult to achieve. In all his work he offers up suggestions for pondering. Some are of course, obvious. Others are more nuanced. He doesn't pretend to know what is good for you. He just opens up his life and says "Hello. This is what I have done for myself and those I love. Maybe there is something here you can benefit from. I hope so. He does not necessarily give advice. That is not his style. He recognizes we are all different and our paths to contentment vary as much as we do one from another."

—Carrol Underwood, Humanitarian

"If you have ever racked your brain in the middle of the night, wondering how to find and keep the love you dream about, you can relax. This book will show you the right questions to ask so your dreams for love can come true. Knowledge is only as powerful as the questions that gave rise to it. Tom Ziemann's heart-felt and honest approach to love will not only show you the right questions to ask, but the answers as well. If you want to find your dream relationship, Creating the Relationship of Your Dreams is one of the best guides around. The amount of wisdom and heart-felt honesty in this book is astounding. Every chapter breathes with the sort of frank discussions and questions that will make love real in your life. So if you have ever yearned to know what the 'real score' with love is, and how to actually create a dream relationship in the current and mostly confusing reality we live in, Tom Ziemann's book is the "no non-sense," trustworthy, and practical guide you've been looking for."

—**Dr. Gary Salyer**, author of *Safe to Love Again: How to Release the Pain of Past Relationships and Create the Love You Deserve*

"Tom Ziemann dives into the grit of love. *Creating the Relationship of Your Dreams* takes us on a journey through the highs and lows of relationship and human potential. Ziemann is personal, raw and honest. Nothing could be more valuable today than the wisdom of love."

—**Richard Silvia**, Activist, Author of *Teach Love* and Founder of #YesRising

"Relationships are the cornerstone of Life. All people require healthy relationships to thrive. We humans spend our lives needlessly trying to perfect ourselves and our relationships. Tom Ziemann insightfully reminds us that for most of us, Life is about awakening to the truth: in order to have healthy, mature relationships we must first learn to love ourselves. *Creating the Relationship of Your Dreams* is a brilliant cornucopia of wisdom!"

—**Jon Satin and Chris Pattay,** The Possibility Coaches: Life, Relationship and Business Coaches.

Authors of: *Living an Inspired, Empowered and Joy-filled Life: 365 Daily Tips to get You There.*
www.PossibilityCoaches.com

"The relationship book I wish I'd had twenty years ago. Tom takes you along his own journey of trials and triumphs to reveal the secret to successful relationships – yourself."
—Tisha Morris, author of *Mind Body Home* and *Clutter Intervention*

"Enjoyed reading the Perennial Wisdom. These are the blocks for healing and how to be open for love. It's a skillful means and following this process with reflection and work on oneself, will heal the blocks to a loving relationship.
This can be a powerful tool for relationship."
—Ondrea Levine, co-author with her Beloved husband, Stephen Levine (who passed in 2016) of *Embracing the Beloved,*

"Another great book, Tom. Picked up the manuscript you sent and read it this afternoon. Fast reader. But, the real truth is, you write so personally, it flows quickly. Great advice and counsel on recognizing that, with any relationship failure, there is a role we all play and, instead of pointing fingers at the other party, going within and recognizing the sometimes puzzling internal stuff that gets in the way of a healthy relationship...well, that's the place to start in order to learn and to grow and to prepare yourself for a more meaningful relationship going forward. Good work Tom."

—**Dr Steve McSwain**, Author, Speaker, Spiritual Teacher

"If you're looking for a definitive, from soup to nuts, no-nonsense, inspiring yet nitty-gritty guide to creating, developing and maintaining a long-term relationship with "The One," then Creating The Relationship of Your Dreams is the book for you!"-

—**Cate Montana, MA**, best-selling author of *The E Word and Apollo & Me.*

"The manuscript is a detailed account of Tom Ziemann's personal journey with which I believe many can relate. References to other works throughout highlight the importance of knowing one's limitations in unfamiliar situations and when to seek assistance in moving through uncharted territories.

I am hopeful your latest creation meets with much success." Blessings.

—**Dr. Shelley Leutschaf PhD, LP**

"A couple of years ago, a former client introduced me to Tom Ziemann. It seemed she felt he and I had some common interests and skills as well as shared meaning in her life. Tom wrote to me and generously shared a complimentary copy of his book *Taming the Anger Dragon: From Pissed Off to Peaceful.* After reading his book, I wanted to meet him. I contacted him and asked him if he would be interested in co-facilitating an anger management workshop with me. Even better, he agreed to let me use part of the title of his book in the name of the workshop. It was such a pleasure working with Tom.

I was pleasantly surprised and honored when Tom followed up by inviting me to review this book. What I like about Tom's approach is his honest appraisal of himself and his willingness to share his authentic self with others. He skillfully shares his experiences in personal stories woven in with down-to-earth, common sense tips on creating and/or building healthy and meaningful relationships. One idea Tom repeatedly emphasizes is our right to choose. I love his discussion about autonomy and the difference between it and independence. Tom's advice about informing ourselves about our values and making choices that support what is important to us is right on. I especially like Tom's discussion of emotional gardening. I frequently tell my clients that building a healthy relationship involves identifying the underlying patterns that repeat themselves and working to develop new and more supportive interactions. Healthy relationships blossom and grow when we nurture them. We must weed and feed our relationships much like we might tend to a garden. I wish Tom's readers love and light as you discover your garden of love and companionship."-

—Darian Slayton Fleming: LCSW, CRC

"As a business consultant who guides people to create the business and life of their dreams, Tom Ziemann's book, *Creating the Relationship of Your Dreams* is in alignment with that goal. It combines one man's story of the pitfalls and perils of self-limiting thoughts with the liberation that occurred when he confronted them, clearing down to the foundation and then rebuilding from the ground up. It offers step by step ideas to bring a partner into your life, sustain a healthy relationship, as well as accepting your life for what it is in the present, whether you are single or in a relationship. I highly recommend this book."

—**Terri Levine**, **PhD** Bestselling author of dozens of titles including "*About To Break: The Path To True Forgiveness*"

"Tom Ziemann walks the talk and lives the life he envisioned through the pages of this amazing book! He is authentic, engaging and I appreciate his approach to relationships. I've learned so much from him! You will, too!"-

—**Sheryl Nelsen Hutton**, *The Self-Help Whisperer*™

"Hi Tom,
I have finished reading the manuscript you emailed me; I have to say that it was very inspiring and encouraging to read. Your words carry the weight of

accumulated experiences and challenges overcome, and that is why your book will be so powerful in its impact upon those who read it. I agree with you, that sometimes we get stuck in a scarcity mindset, rather than one of abundant blessings. But blessings are all around us, all we need to do is accept and enjoy them, in heartfelt gratitude towards the one who has bestowed them upon us. They can be found in the sounds of birds sitting in the trees, on the lakes and ponds, yes, we are truly all connected.

Your words, will uplift, those struggling to get their relationships back on the straight and narrow, as within its pages, lies a treasure trove of beneficial ideas and practical solutions for people who want to evolve their relationships to higher levels of enjoyment and exploration. Where you speak of life's meaning, in your book, one could say that yours, like mine is to reach out to others with a spirit of kindness and compassion. In this we are very much alike, in that we both have a heart for encouraging our fellow brothers and sisters, through the words we write.

Truth is, as men and women, we often allow things to divide us, to separate us, and to introduce hostility and bitterness into the relationships, and friendships we both have together. We need to realize that together we are like two equal but separate halves of a rectangle, one is not complete if one half, is not joined by the other half. Thus, we are without unity, when there is no unity there is division, and neither side will benefit from this, here are some words that you might like to use.

*Men should not be above Women, that they should be the master.
*Men should not be below Women, that." they should be the slave.
*Men should not be in front of Women; that they should be the leader.
*Men should not be behind Women, that they should be subordinate to them,
But Men should always stand side by side with Women.

*Women should not be above Men, that they should be the master.
*Women should not be below Men, that they should be their slaves.
*Women should not be in front of Men, that they should be the leader
*Women should not be behind Men, that they should be subordinate to them.
But Women should always stand side by side with Men.

I appreciate your kindness in allowing me to be the first one to read your
manuscript. It was a privilege my friend, and all the best to you. Thanks Tom."

—**Marcus Scriven,** Writer and Humanist

"Tom does a deep dive into the world of relationships, and provides countless insights, tips and ideas to help you find the love you truly desire and deserve. And he does it while being vulnerable and real about his own struggles to find the same. His book is a good tool for anyone seriously seeking to create a meaningful relationship."
—**Austin Vickers Esquire,** Writer and Producer, *People v. The State of Illusion*

"Tom Ziemann's latest book on relationships isn't just another book of platitudes; it is a "how to" for those who really aren't sure how to even start to find or mend a relationship. Tom helps you walk through what might have gone wrong in past relationships, how to not make the same mistakes again, and how to revitalize a relationship that may have lost its spark. Using examples from his own life and input from others, Tom never speaks down to his readers nor does he ever say that his is the only way. Even if you are in a happy, long-term relationship, you can find some ways to make your relationship more rewarding. I recommend it."-
—**Brenda Braden, Lead Attorney**- City of Tualatin, Oregon, Retired

"We have 2 ears and 1 mouth to listen more than we speak. Otherwise we would have 2 mouths and 1 ear. You provide an in-depth approach to learning about ourselves through understanding others, but more importantly, the psychological analysis of ourselves. When truthful we can truly find the path to our authentic selves. This book will help many. Thank you."

—Terrance Ellis- Actor

"Tom lays out a path to understanding what it takes to create partnerships that thrive. Learning how to be a better you so you can become a better we is powerful but takes work. Thanks for sharing your journey and guide to get here as we can all use these insights in our relationships to keep them fresh, happy and healthy."

—Jenny Smith Insurance Agency, Inc. Owner/President

"Tom Ziemann is raw, honest, and endearing and you'll feel like he's sitting in a coffee shop with you and sharing between hot, frothy sips as he shares his relationship experiences and valuable insights to help the reader navigate their way through understanding and possibly obtaining a connection perfect for them."

—Lisa Hardwick Best Selling Author and Publisher of SDJ Productions

"Awesome insightful read, once again Tom has addressed the very core of self in relationships and life on life terms therein. As in Toms past novels I again found doorways which I did not recognize until I began reading deep within the pages of this new edition. As always the writings not only illuminate but offer custom fit tools as well within each chapter. I feel comfortable in applying these pages to my life and love therein simply because I have witnessed first-hand his wonderful relationship with his wife Michelle."

Sincerely,
—DWBright, Lightraiser & Healer

"With insight & depth, Tom uses his own journey & lessons to provide the reader with a guide for relationship happiness & success."
—Kate Olson, Hypnotherapist, Host of Soul Fire Wisdom on Soul Fire Radio

DEDICATION

This book was written for those looking to create their dream relationship and for others currently in a relationship looking for suggestions to keep it fresh. It is also for those looking for ways to gain a better understanding of who they are, thereby creating a greater harmonious relationship within themselves. By doing so they open the floodgates of possibilities and even deeper, more rewarding relationships.

FOREWORD
BY DR. CHRISTIAN CONTE

You don't have to have been married for 50 plus years to know what it takes to be married for 50 plus years. The answers - the keys to successful relationships are not rocket science, but they are, in actuality, science. Knowing and doing are of course two different entities and knowing what it takes to have a successful relationship is vastly different than actually living out what you know is right. There is a formula for successful relationships, and it begins with getting to know yourself.

Your words and actions play a huge role in your relationships, but so too, does your energy. The energy you bring every day to your relationships impacts them in profound ways, and as long as you focus on what others can do differently to satisfy you, you will miss what you can do to contribute to a healthy relationship.

Although anyone can point out how others need to change or how you need to find others who fall in line with the way you think, feel, believe or behave, the more accurate reality is that we are not in control of the outside world, only ourselves, and the more we demand that others change to fit our needs, the more we spiral down the path of narcissism, and worse, the kind of control that leads to abuse at its worst, and miserable relationships at best. To be with others, then, begins with knowing yourself; but of course it does not end there.

Relationships are about connecting with others. The key is in that phrase: "Connecting with others." That is not to say "controlling" others or "manipulating" others, but it is to focus on connecting with them. To connect with others authentically requires that we take a deep dive within ourselves, get to understand how others experience us, and to work constantly at neither losing ourselves nor demanding that our partners become ourselves. That balance is created through awareness.

What you bring to your relationships has a profound impact on them. In other words, if your energy goes up and down with your partner, if your responses are merely reactions, or if you struggle to accept the differences your partner brings, then your relationships are likely to be as sturdy as ones that are built on shaky ground.

If, conversely, you can put your entire effort into learning about yourself, your defense mechanisms, and the ways in which you unrealistically demand that your partner lives according to your magical world of "shoulds" (or what I call the "cartoon world"), then you have a real chance to both align your expectations with reality and create a relationship that is fulfilling and lasting.

In Creating the Relationship of Your Dreams, Tom Ziemann shares the wisdom that he's learned through his successes, and perhaps more importantly, his failures, and he compiles information that has helped him ultimately find peace in his relationships. His message is important: You can only control yourself, it's wise to make clear, achievable relationship goals, and above all, relationships take effort. The effort, however, is best spent on looking inward, not in trying to control your partner or make your partner into some "ready-made" puppet who thinks, feels, believes and behaves how you choose.

You are the only constant in all of your relationships. The more you get to know yourself, the healthier your relationships become. Instead of assessing your relationships in terms of what your partner can do for you, go inward to learn about yourself, and then emerge with a level of consciousness that allows you to not just have a great partner, but to be a great partner.

Sending everyone who sees this, and everyone who doesn't, much peace.

Christian Conte, Ph.D. Author, *Walking Through Anger*

INTRODUCTION

When I started this project, my dear friend Marc asked me a question. He is a very rational thinker. He doesn't sugarcoat answers either. Over the years, he has posed very tough questions to me.

He said, "Tom, with literally thousands of books on relationships already written, why yours? What will be different about it?" I smiled and said, "You know, that's a great question, I'm glad you asked it. As you know I have been researching relationships for decades; as well as many years of writing on the subject and connecting with readers through my blogs. This led me to explore the many habits, beliefs, and experiences of others. It makes me believe that I have a highly informative book to share."

Some incredible books gave me wonderful insight and have made me ponder what a good relationship is. *The 5 Love Languages* is one of my favorites. That said, I hadn't found one book that encompassed all the aspects for which I was looking for under one cover that fully resonated with me."

Without hesitation he said: "Go on".

"I continued, "Having been in many failed relationships, I wanted to share where I fell short so others might glean the lessons without having to repeat my mistakes themselves. I would include things that worked for me. Being extremely careful not to suggest my ideas were right or the only way to achieve Relationship Perfection or Nirvana. Nor would they be Pollyannaish or pie in the sky and unachievable. Simply put, these thoughts would be easy to relate to without any complicated psychological jargon. These ideas could be understood on both an intellectual and emotional level simultaneously.

No relationship is ever perfect; all have different challenges and levels of uniqueness. In my book, I wanted to address the entire animal from start to finish.

Seeking out a meaningful relationship, one that fits well with the reader's wants. Sharing tools to help them choose the right one, that will work based on what they desire. What they want and need to feel fulfilled.

Knowing who they are "completely" makes this possible; helping them evaluate past relationships, what worked and what didn't.

Appraising their current relationship, is it working for both of them? And delve deep into a potential relationship, will it stand the test of time? Are you both compatible?

Moreover, sharing suggestions on how to keep a relationship alive, learning how to share one's thoughts constructively and even fight fair concerning conflicts.

I am neither a Psychologist nor licensed therapist; therefore I have enlisted the guidance of internationally known, bestselling book author, columnist, and speaker, Reverend Edie Weinstein MSW, LSW as one as my creative consultants. Based on her expertise, numerous blogs, interviews, and countless hours of working firsthand with clients, it is my fervent hope the reader will find that she adds credibility to the book.

In addition, I have called on renowned Relationship Coach, Certified Marriage Coach and Strategic Interventionist Jennifer Blankl to give this project even greater depth and more impactful tools for its readers. Both of them are well respected, intelligent women who would help round out my thoughts by adding the female perspective.

Some of the chapters are from blogs that I have written; they will add value, deeper meaning, and understanding to the whole of the book which will make sense when its messages are fully digested, pondered, and put into practice.

I will share my personal story of past failed relationships; what I learned and how it helped elevate me to finding the love of my life, my wife Michelle.

For me, I liken the death of someone I loved, a dear friend or cherished pet to a tender relationship that was lost. Pain is pain. Some hurt more than others. One must grieve in their way and time if one is to come to terms with it.

There are no specific, hard, and fast rules for how long it lasts. My thinking also tells me the depth of the relationship will act as the barometer of the duration of your pain.

Additionally, I have added wonderful thoughts from focus groups; their practical ideas about successful relationships replete with ways to implement them should they resonate with you, as well as pertinent things to be aware of.

In closing, regardless of the reason, may this book be of service, whether you picked it up to get some suggestions on how to create that dream relationship you've desired, perhaps the title intrigued you, or you picked it up out of curiosity. Maybe you already have a good relationship and are simply looking for ideas to help keep it fresh.

In the chapters ahead the thoughts shared are beneficial in any type of relationship, especially the one with yourself. Being amenable to new ideas opens the door to possibilities. Even if you completely disagree with some of the premises put forth, that's good. It means you know yourself. You WIN!

Although I am a heterosexual, cis-gender man who is sharing his own journey, everything offered in this book is applicable to individuals and couples of any gender presentation or sexual orientation.

Please join me now on your journey to creating the relationship you've been dreaming about.

Much love and warmth,

Thomas E Ziemann

PART ONE:

LIVING, LOVING AND LEARNING ABOUT RELATIONSHIPS

CHAPTER 1:

I HAD A DREAM

"You alone are the judge of your worth
and your goal is to discover infinite worth in yourself,
no matter what anyone else thinks."
~Deepak Chopra

I had a dream, but not quite as iconic as the great Martin Luther King Jr's incredible speech. Certainly, Dr. King's mind-blowing talk will go down as one of the greatest demonstrations for freedom in the history of mankind.

Mine was of a dream relationship that had always eluded me. One where I could be 100% myself and still be accepted by my mate. A relationship that made me feel alive long after the initial sexual attraction and urges had passed. One that would make me get up in the morning and long to spend time with my love. One that reminded me of a cheesy Hallmark movie where my beautiful lady would swoon over me and make me feel like a real man, without having to prove it to anyone. One who would appreciate my sensitive, well in-tune emotional side. One where I would be cherished and loved just because. Cared for and nurtured. One in which I could speak my mind without having to worry I would hurt her feelings or be misunderstood. One that I wouldn't be embarrassed about being with, that I could take home to Mother. One that would help me grow emotionally and never call me out in front of others when I screwed up or bring my past shortcomings up when I irritated her, or we were in a spat. A classy, smart, funny, beautiful, spiritually minded, politically Liberal, nonjudgmental, animal lover who would also love my cats and would get along with both of my grown daughters. Not perfect, but perfect for me. One who could handle my INTENSITY, anger issues, perfectionistic, A.D.H.D idiosyncrasies, OCD inclinations, to mention but a few of my characteristics.

Tall order right? I'll bet some guys are gagging right now.

Well, after many years of failed, lackluster relationships, and working on myself, I eventually found "The One".

The main point is that it would have never happened had I not done the inner work. Rather than worrying daily about finding her, I had to focus on becoming the right person. To become my own best friend. Comfortable spending time with just me. To love myself, more than anyone else. I am guessing some reading that sentence will cringe.

I am not referring to a narcissistic self-absorption. More of a full acceptance of who I was, what I have become, and who I would strive to be.

Of course, the secret was getting to know who I was and accepting myself completely and being willing to pay the price. Going for what I genuinely wanted to be was what needed to happen. Don't kid yourself and think all this is easy. Quality relationships rarely happen without effort on our part. They take time to create, however, the payoff can be huge!

In the chapters ahead, I will share how it happened for me and many others so that you too can "rub your inner magic lamp" and create a magical relationship if that's your goal.

Believing that you are worthy of such an exalted and esteemed relationship is crucial to your success. Being

100% committed to the belief that you have a right like anyone else to experience a dream relationship is the oil that lubricates the gears of possibilities.

Once you have that mastered, working on all your issues will help bring your mate into your life. A bonus is that you will be maturing emotionally and spiritually along your path.

You must be willing to see yourself in an unflattering light without judgment, only acknowledging you had these tendencies and you're working to alleviate them. Next step is to be willing to fail, as you put yourself out there. Making the effort to meet someone takes time. Being proactive and patient is crucial.

Taking the chance on relationships you initially thought you would never get or felt worthy of before. Let your future mate decide that.

Don't try to attempt to commit all the ideas mentioned here to memory. Every suggestion will be shared in much greater detail as the chapters unfold.

While most of the chapters and sections are short, they boast some of the finest beneficial, practical, and heartfelt ideas I have found thus far. We are an extremely time-poor society; we want immediate results. It was my purpose to keep this book simple and to the point, so that the reader can put the ideas to practical use in their daily lives.

What dreams have you had about your 'ideal' relationship?

Does it feel attainable rather than only being part of a fantasy?

Are you ready to turn the page and write your own story?

CHAPTER 2:

REALITY

"Our destiny is not written for us,
but by us."
~Barack Obama

During my adolescent years I hadn't had much success with any type of meaningful relationships or deep friendships. I hated myself. My issues were many; I had low self-esteem, seen as "the neighborhood pussy" that got his lily-white ass kicked regularly until the 9th grade. My relationship with both my parents was dysfunctional.

Truth be told, my parents had a relationship of convenience; any romance they may have once shared fizzled out long before I was old enough to understand what a loving relationship meant. They weren't even friends. Mutual tolerance was the closest thing to being buddies they shared. I cannot fathom being married to or involved with someone who wasn't also a great friend.

My mother stayed home and took care of the house, while my father brought in the money. Sadly, I cannot remember a single kind gesture by either or any romantic exchanges. Not once did I ever see them kiss, hold hands, leave nice notes for each other or do anything together other than bowl on a league the same night and come watch me compete at swim meets. Sure we had family outings; occasional picnics and a few family vacations were the extent of their spending time together. Neither had developed any deep friendships outside their dismal, lackluster, loveless marriage.

Chivalry wasn't a concept my father had vaguely a clue about. Not once did he bring home flowers, hold the door for her, or even compliment my mother. They didn't sleep in the same room either.

This was a wakeup call for me. I vowed I would be different.

While I did have some "girl friends" through High School, nothing came of it. Kissing and heavy petting for sure, but no real connections. To make matters worse, I was a big mouth know-it- all which didn't help me in the popular realm. I was my own worst enemy. No one likes a braggart. Plus, I sucked at most sports.

All during school, I witnessed what I perceived to be meaningful relationships. Most kids appeared to have quality family lives and connected with their siblings and parents.

I knew something was missing. In between classes, I saw the entire handholding, note passing, and walking arm in arm in school routine between those high school sweethearts who seemed to love each other. Not to mention the school dances and roller-skating parties that I missed out on. I was the wallflower. Nobody gave me the time of day, and when they did, I pushed them away with my ego, intensity, and weirdness. I thought that anybody who'd wanna be with me must be a loser. I felt like a dismal failure.

I had a ton of crushes on the hot chicks, but I felt they were too good for me. How could I possibly date one of them? What did I have to offer them? I didn't even have a car, let alone any money. There was always this nagging, loneliness that followed me like a dark cloud. **I was hating my life for sure**.

I couldn't wait to graduate High School and move back to Chicago as my family moved us out to the suburbs when I was at the end of 5th grade.

45

That day finally happened. I moved into my grandmother's house; she had given me a flat in her basement.

How cool was that? A 17-year-old who had his own apartment! I came and went as I pleased. This was the beginning of my early life as an adult. Yet, it was short-lived as my grandmother's house burnt to the ground not long after.

It was one of those make it or break it moments. Luckily for me, a record shop owner where I was helping out on the weekends asked me if I wanted to rent a room in the building he owned. It was a no brainer. I did so and then I found a job and my life and financial means suddenly improved. While living in the three-story brownstone on Chicago's Northside, I met a mentor who changed my life. His name was George Spaulding. A bright, witty, and funny man in his 70s. Super generous and he took a shine to me, flaws, and all. We started a wonderful friendship.

It's where I learned about life, people, music, and culture. Spaulding never judged me; he knew I meant well, only that I needed emotional maturity. He never scolded me either, even when I was a total A' hole. He spent time with me, sharing life experiences. He used the Socratic Method when teaching which made me ponder what he was trying to convey and allowed me to come to my own conclusions. During our time together, I started to become aware that my life and who I was, mattered.

While all this was fine and dandy, I knew in my heart, I wasn't doing anything with my life professionally and decided to enlist in the Navy. He supported the idea wholeheartedly and we remained friends for many years after until he died suddenly. The loss I felt was incalculable as was the gratitude for the tutelage he gave me. A second chance on life, if you will. He instilled in me a genuine desire for knowledge, an unquenchable thirst to find perspective on every subject.

He always urged me to go to the library and educate myself. He told me to read all the books and know something about everything. He taught me that you didn't have to know everything, just know how to ask intelligent questions. He helped my self-esteem by never forcing anything on me, always led by example, or by asking questions. He helped me to find the confidence I lacked as a child. He told me that he believed in me. That one day I would accomplish amazing things. That I was good enough as I was, and that a relationship didn't make the man, instead, it exposed who he was to himself if he took the time to examine.

You may be wondering why I shared that story. My reason is simple. This was a person who gave me a chance; he gave me the ability to start liking myself.

I had no idea how much his lessons would benefit me and follow me for the rest of my life.

In case you didn't have a mentor early in life, now you can experience vicariously what I gleaned, thereby helping to supplement your life with some of the common themes he shared.

That I mattered.

That I could become someone.

That I was worthy of creating a loving relationship.

That there were kind people in the world that expected nothing in return.

That I was good enough just as I was and could do things to improve.

Now I had the confidence to believe I was capable of doing things.

My self-education continued, as well as meeting another mentor, my first martial arts instructor who shared his love of meditation. That set me off on a whole separate path of spirituality which I have followed me ever since.

Fast forward....20 years later, I am a father of two beautiful daughters in a lackluster marriage I wasn't happy with. Even with all my book reading, I still hadn't grown enough emotional maturity to realize what I wanted. Yes, I was financially stable. Yes, I finally found a good woman who loved me. However due to anger issues which I had never dealt with, it caused massive damage that was not repairable. We were divorced 15 years after we said: "I do". Mostly my fault, I take FULL RESPONSIBILITY for my actions. I was an idiot and have no one to blame but myself for what happened. I needed to do much more inner work.

The silver lining is that Shannon and I have remained friends.

I learned many things from her and value her wisdom.

Did you have a mentor growing up?

If so, what did you learn from this person?

If not, it is never too late.

CHAPTER 3:

THE CONVERSATION

*"The future belongs to those who believe
in the beauty of their dreams."*
~ Eleanor Roosevelt

The pinnacle of my life, in the relationship realm was an unexpected conversation with my first mentor Spaulding. The one that seemed vivid, lucid and thought provoking. I remember it as if it had happened yesterday. It occurred during my least favorite time of the year; that dour, gray, melancholy period between Christmas and New Year's Day. Oregon's foreboding overcast skies are never kind during that season. Many people, me included, become depressed with heavy clouds day after day. Usually I could sublimate my bored and lonely feelings by playing the "host with the most" as I was fond of entertaining my friends four times weekly. I put out lavish spreads of stinky cheese, bread and butter pickles, black and green olives, Ritz crackers, etc. I jammed new music perhaps they hadn't heard and chewed the fat. Top shelf Tequilas made their way to the table during these loud soirees. I had Pandora permeating through Klipsch speakers playing different rock band music that was eerily similar. It was 2:31 in the afternoon and I had already popped my second Stella Artois into my favorite University of Oregon frosty mug. I was drinking more heavily than usual and had slapped on 10 extra holiday pounds. I felt like a fat Hobbit. My cats could always tell when my depression had worsened. They would hang near me in the front room. The only light visible was coming from the Onkyo stereo. I was sitting in my self-created mire of despondency, self-loathing, and pity. I felt like a total loser. I kept questioning myself, WTF happened?

The next song only exacerbated my mood. America's super hit *Lonely People* wafted out, the notes spilling all over the front room Oriental rugs. I have heard this song hundreds of times, however, I intently listened to every word uttered with astonishment and awe.

It was the essence of this 1970s song that had revealed a truth just for my ears which was a dagger straight to my heart, so I thought at that second. The lyrics go:

"This is for all the lonely people, thinking that life has passed them by."

My body ached as I heard that poignant prose. Tears were welling up in my eyes as I greedily gulped my beer; like a parched sailor who'd just returned from a long WEST-PAC cruise in the Indian Ocean, out at sea too long.

The next verse seemed to give me some comfort.

"Don't give up until you drink from the silver cup. And ride that highway in the sky."

Man, I had already gone down the path of the suicidal thought and it wasn't something I wanted to relive.

The next verse hit me like being run over by The Great Chicago Bear Lineman Dick Butkus.

"This is for all the single people, thinking that love has left them dry."

By this time, I was experiencing a frothy frenzy of torrid emotions tormented by the coldness of those telling, chilling words. They cut right to the bone. I immediately turned off the stereo.

I was weeping like a baby. These last five years had been supremely lonely and mournful. My Anger Dragon within kept fanning the self-doubt thoughts flames as I asked, "What the hell happened to me? Why did I do to deserve this? Why have I acted like such an A' hole in my relationships?" I screwed up the most important ones, with my ex-wife, Shannon, daughters Caitlin and Kelsey, and some long-term friendships. My Ego wasn't acting too proud right now. ARRRRRRRRRRRRRRRRRRRRRGGGGGGGGGGGG GGGGGG!

I must have dozed off for a bit, but when I opened my bloodshot eyes, sitting next to me was Spaulding, looking youthful again. Oddly, he was wearing the same clothes he had on at the last supper we shared. He bought me dinner at one of his favorite restaurants, Ann Sather's on Belmont on the Northside of Chicago. It was a marvelous meal.

I wasn't sure if I was in a deep REM state experiencing hypnagogic delusions or if his ghost had come back to haunt me. When I dream, I find that I am unable to control things that don't make sense, and instead I just accept them.

He reached over to me, touched my shoulder, and said, "Thomas, (He called me Thomas when he had something deep to share) I've been watching you. I have felt your pain." This was so real, I was dumbfounded. My words were incoherent and since I couldn't speak articulately, I just listened. He said, "You are gonna be okay." His voice was soothing, exactly what I needed to hear. He said that I made mistakes as everyone else had. "Quit beating yourself up. You got yourself into this mess and you can make it better." At this point I felt electrified and curious to learn more.

That's when our conversation went deep.

He asked the following questions with the caveat that he didn't want me to answer, only to ponder them and take to heart what he said and think carefully about my responses before verbalizing them.

He spoke slowly and with clarity.

What hurt me?

Why was I so sad?

What have I done to get myself where I am now?

Knowing what I know today, what would have I done differently?

What have I learned from my 1st marriage?

What behaviors will I make to change in my current situation?

What negative beliefs am I carrying that are holding me back?

What will make my next relationship better?

What do I need to feel fulfilled?

What did I envision would be different next time?

What things am I willing to give up?

Am I willing to make a daily effort to bring a rewarding relationship to fruition?

Did I feel worthy of having a dream relationship?

What resources do I have and where can I get the things I need?

What will make my next relationship the dream one I have always wanted?

Finally had I BECOME the person I was seeking?

And just like that, he hugged me, said he loved me and POOF…. his image appeared to dissipate into thin air, like vapor rising from my Koi pond.

Suddenly I felt as I had been resurrected. It was as if I had been lying on a hospital operating table, a heart defibrillator attached to my chest which was sending 1000 volts into my body. I was indeed awake. I looked up the clock and it was only 2:47. Just a few moments had passed, when it had seemed like hours. My beer was still cold, with condensation kissing the outside of my go-to glass.

Was I dreaming? Had Spaulding visited me? My electrified mind was racing. I know from experience to write down every detail which I can remember from dreams so I can glean their subtle, cryptic messages.

I wasn't feeling sorry for myself anymore since I now had a road map.

Have you had dreams that were so vivid, that you thought you were awake?

Have you written them down so you can remember them later?

What do you imagine would happen if you took your dreams to heart and used them to actually create the life of your dreams and desires?

Chapter 4:

My Decision

*"I am not a product of my circumstances.
I am a product of my decisions."*
~ Stephen Covey

My body was still buzzing from the top of my
balding head to my tingling toes. Spaulding's visit (or
my subconscious dream of him) sharing his wisdom
helped catapult me out of the depths of despondency.
This was huge because while I knew something deep
down was wrong I wasn't ready to face it and hadn't
wanted to experience the pain of reality. Kind of like a
Band-Aid, it hurts a hell of a lot more to gently pull it
off as opposed to just ripping it off quickly and then it's
over. While my inner work had just begun, much of

the self-imposed angst I was feeling was lifted. Now I was using my pain as fuel.

I quickly grabbed some paper and a pen. I jotted down every question Spaulding had posed to me.

It took some time to answer his queries, however now I had captured them and could take the time required to ponder them deeply and create a plan to alleviate my pain and potentially create my Dream Relationship.

What hurt me?

Ultimately it was Me who hurt Me... my emotional immaturity, my out of control ego, my vengeful nature, my need to be right, my inability to forgive my ex-wife's perceived trespasses, my pig-headedness was only intensified with the deep- seated anger issues which I had not yet learned to control at that point.

I had a scorched earth policy as it pertained to people who hurt my feelings. I had not learned or wanted for that matter to let certain experiences go. These silly things added to my suffering, not the people I held responsible for hurting me. In my earlier life, I felt like I was Charlie Brown. Seemed like everyone took great pleasure in making my life a living hell. I was teased, constantly picked on, tormented, ridiculed, bullied, belittled, and berated by the local kids. It probably didn't help that I acted a little strange and at times perfumed the stench of urine as I was still wetting the bed. This was a sad fact and rumors about it followed me until I graduated high school.

That coupled with being a person of smaller stature and not knowing how to fight or even protect myself made me an easy target for the bullies and hooligans of Eastview Jr High. I used to get my ass kicked at least once a week. One time I was walking down the hall there, minding my own business and this punk decided to kick me in the mouth with his cowboy boots on. Warm blood oozed out my mouth, however my pride hurt even more. I hated my life, having to fear for my survival.

As the old saying goes; when seeking revenge, you should dig two graves. It's extremely painful to realize that I was alone after my failed marriage. It hurt to know that I was ultimately responsible for its failure as well as the hurt I had caused to my ex and children. Truth be told, they weren't all that surprised when they heard we were getting a divorce as they had witnessed years of bickering.

While it sucked royally to finally admit my part in our debacle, it was strangely freeing at the same time, as it allowed me to come to grips with it and begin the healing part; to begin forgiving myself.

It took some time; but I am happy to report, my ex and I have remained good friends. I have re-established loving relationships with both my daughters. All this was possible because I was willing to see myself in an unflattering light and accepted responsibility. Examining where I fell short helped me to plan to fix my future and resolve not to repeat the same immature mistakes.

All of a sudden a flash of inspiration hit me that I had it all wrong as it pertained to Seeking the Dream Relationship. To have it, I needed to become the man who would create it. I would accomplish this by shedding past illogical beliefs and actions and strive from that moment on to live up to the things I knew would propel me to be a better man. I would attempt to learn everything there was to know about successful relationships.

Why was I so sad?

This was answered in my last response. I would merely add I was sad because I didn't live up to my full potential. That I didn't forgive. I felt like a complete and utter failure.

What have I done to get myself where I am now?

Spaulding's visit certainly made me cognizant of my current situation. He helped me look at where I was and accept it, which is something I wasn't willing to beforehand. Now I had a road map to healing.

Knowing what I know today, what would have I done differently?

I would have worked on myself; not expecting that another person would fulfill me or create inner happiness for me. I would have acted more patient, compassionate, and loving. More open to the other's perspective.

I would have considered my ex's feelings, trying to see her point of view as opposed to thinking I was always right. I would have learned to communicate better and not taken things she said so personally. I would have taken time daily to work on our relationship rather than assuming that was her job. My thoughts ran along the lines of "Why should I be fully engaged if she isn't doing her part?" I would have allowed my children to state their opinions as opposed to always having the last word. I maintained an attitude of, "I'm your older and wiser father therefore I know best.

What have I learned from my first marriage?

That I was too emotionally immature to take the effort to make it work. That while I was an adequate provider, it takes more than merely bringing home the bacon to feed a marriage. Realizing your partner has her own needs, desires, thoughts, wants and goals and how to support her are crucial to enhancing the relationship. That it takes daily work for real happiness and growth. That we both will change during our time together which is normal. Figuring out how to navigate life's curveballs and the other's changing needs are paramount to sustaining a healthy marriage. Perhaps learning how to fight fair and improve communication. Listening to each other. That I didn't have to shoulder the burden for every issue we experienced.

What behaviors will I make to change in my current situation?

In addition to what I already wrote, I would need to grow up. I would be required to learn what it takes to become a more rounded and emotionally intelligent man. I would have to control my anger and become much more adept in communication skills. I would need to learn to forgive on the spot. I would be called on to love myself and quit looking elsewhere to find it.

What negative beliefs am I carrying that are holding me back?

Too many to mention, including my unhealthy ego, lack of forgiveness, holding on to negative thoughts, all those suppressed, undealt with emotions; those nagging negative self-talk conversations pulsated constantly through my head; "You aren't good enough, you're a loser. You'll never be able to support yourself let alone a family. You screw up most things that you care about," and many more. These deep-seated, negative unfounded beliefs fired my Anger Dragon's flames which consumed me. I had allowed my anger to control my life which held me back.

What will make my next relationship better?

The easy answer is I will make it better because I will be a different man. I will learn tools to become the person I was seeking, and it would happen. Much of this will come from looking for a partner who wasn't perfect, simply perfect for me. One where our communication would be excellent. Where I would know her Love languages and act accordingly.

What do I need to feel fulfilled?

To fully love me. A dream relationship only adds to my life.

What did I envision would be different next time?

Since I will evolve and grow, my next relationship will be more fulfilling. I see a beautiful, kind, compassionate, caring lady who will help me grow and mature even more. Once I master and embody all those attributes, I will attract what I wish.

What things am I willing to give up?

My anger, my need to always be right, my perfectionistic attitude, My lack of awareness and compassion, as well as my Ego.

Am I willing to make a daily effort to bring a rewarding relationship to fruition?

Having been out of the dating game for many years, I would have to commit daily to improving myself; reading everything I could get my hands on and putting myself out there even when I didn't feel like doing so.

Did I feel worthy of having a dream relationship?

For the first time in my adult life, I felt I truly was.

What resources do I have and where can I get the things I need?

Having been in the Success Motivation industry, I possessed a great number of the bestselling classics on relationships that I would need to re-read or listen to again to reacquaint myself with their sage advice. It was refreshing to hear Dr. David Viscott, Erich Fromm, Eckhart Tolle, M. Scott Peck, Mark Nepo, Nathaniel Branden, Leo Buscaglia, and Gary Chapman once again, this time with new ears, and an unfettered mind replete with an open heart. I would have long talks with people I respected, such as therapists, doctors, psychologists, and other professionals to pick their brains. Also, seeking out new messengers daily like Dr. Christian Conte and don Miguel Ruiz Jr. to get their spin on things. I would pose questions on my Facebook and social media sites to get a wide swath of other opinions I may not have considered.

What will make my next relationship the dream one I have always wanted?

To reiterate, I would become the person I was seeking. I would give myself the love I was searching for. I would fully accept myself. I would create it.

I speak from many years of unrequited love. Never got the emotional love from my parents I deeply desired, (rejoice if you had such an amazing father) nor the deep romantic love I've always wished for.

Romantic Love is a crazy thing… you love him, he loves her, and she loves another. It's a sad fact that most of us have dealt with it. Engaging in sex is important and also the easy part. My goal would be to search for a woman who matched me on all levels. I want to desire her completely, mind, and body.

I want to be with the woman who I was just was physical with and still delighted to be with her afterward or I felt something is missing. Kind of cheapens it for me, although that doesn't sound like a typical man saying that, right? LOL

Far better to be alone to wish I were had been my mantra since my divorce 10 years prior. Still I had faith and hope that She was out there. My advice to anyone would be to not to look for perfection, rather look for someone perfect for you. Someone who sees your faults and loves you anyway. Someone you can be completely honest with, can act unconventional with and have them still desire you. This is expected by one's partner as well, methinks.

I had an epiphany...I was looking to creating an evolving relationship; these deep kinds of relationships involve two committed, loving people living a human experience together with all its perfect imperfections who are moving forward together.

Finally had I BECOME the person I was seeking?

I had a long way to go but I was on the road less traveled.

Are you willing to become the person you are seeking?

What would it take to embody the values you have?

How have you picked yourself up after leaving an unhealthy relationship?

CHAPTER 5:

EMOTIONAL GARDENING

"Emotional reactions will always pop up and have power over you until you deal with the unresolved feats that hide underneath them."
~ don Miguel Ruiz Jr.

I am known by my close friends as "Mr. Hardcore Gardener" I've been an addicted enthusiast for well over 25 years. I take distinct pleasure in having one of the greenest lawns on the block. For decades, I have shared the secrets if you will, tips and tonics with many people on how to rejuvenate their lawns. In some cases, I've helped them do the thatching, core aeration, augmentation for their particular soil, choosing correct fertilizers, advised and suggested the best lawn seed to purchase, and voila, in just a few short months, they too had lawns to be envied.

Additionally, I have subsequently created my own "Zen Gardens" on both of my properties; my "Taoist sanctuary"; special private place of respite, tranquility, meditation, and reflection. Feeding our beautiful Koi is one of the things I ardently enjoy doing during the active months.

I am awestruck by the similarities between one's garden and emotional state. Both require cultivation and care if they are to prosper. A basic understanding of such has helped me to "right my ship" as it were.

During Spaulding's visit, it became quite apparent my emotional soil had been sorely neglected and required immediate attention. I wasn't looking forward to the arduous task which lay ahead of me, however for things to change, I had to.

Here's what I did…

The first step I needed to take was to assess my situation.

Using complete self-honesty and being willing to see myself in an unflattering light allowed me to accept who I would become. I had to forgive my past behaviors and flaws and began immediately to rectify them as I started to weed them out.

Once I completed this, I compiled my to-do list which I could follow and implement immediately.

Rototilling- Augmenting and turning the soil; turning over a new leaf springs to mind, a wonderful metaphor used since the 16th century. In other words, improving one's conduct creates a change for the better. Being willing to look honestly at your life, without judgment or excuses and then taking the steps required to rectify said issues is the key to meaningful, lasting changes.

Fertilizing- Plants require specific nutrients, adding proper nourishment for the soil will help increase the yield and facilitate the overall health of the plant.

For me, this step was akin to getting back to basics. Re-reading/listening to the incredible books which I already had in my library was merely part of my daily fertilizing. Next, I scoured Google and Good Reads for highly rated books on relationships as well as asking people what their favorite relationship book was and why they liked it. I kept a detailed list and slowly whittled it down, I checked off the books I read and added others as they were suggested. Many of the ideas I found beneficial are melded into this book. Watching YouTube videos, TED Talks and live online programs all helped round out my ongoing research.

Planting seeds- Choosing wisely the best quality seeds will enhance the yield of any garden. Best seeds have higher genetic purity which translates into higher germination, vigor, and stamina. The seeds I have chosen for my relationship was finally knowing who I was and endeavoring to become a better man. What I wanted and needed in a relationship as well as the teachers, tools (books and CDs) to educate myself on what all those things were to help me grow.

Key point: When we know exactly what we want and are willing to pay the price to get it, we stand an excellent chance of winning. I have always believed that all plant life possesses special intelligence.

The first time I heard this it blew my mind, that when we add our saliva directly on the seed before we plant it in the dirt, something unexplainable occurs. The seed will absorb our DNA; it becomes part of its blueprint!

Yes, by doing so, you become a key component of its unique genetic code. If the plant is edible, it becomes "Super Food". How it somehow knows how to add and decipher our DNA just boggles the mind.

Watering- Plants need adequate moisture, not too much or too little. Like getting plenty of fluids, receiving what we need in a relationship is the ultimate goal. Knowing ourselves and our partner's needs help us get things we both deem necessary for our mutual satisfaction and inner wellbeing. Watering your relationship with love, time, and compassion makes for a fulfilling one.

PH levels in the garden are incredibly important to maintaining it, keeping an eye on the soil is a must. Soil pH has indirect yet far-reaching effects on plants. Avoidance of two extremes is crucial. In simple terms, the pH scale goes from 1-14 a pH of 1 is highly acidic and a pH of 14 is highly alkaline. Too low can yield low effects on the overall health of the leaves, they turn yellow and stunts the growth of the plant. Too high pH levels increase its toxicity.

Therefore a pH of 6.5 is just about right for most gardens since most plants thrive in the 6.0 to 7.0 (slightly acidic to neutral) ranges. So where am I going with this? I liken this analogy to living The Middle Way, that of moderation. In Buddhism, it's referred to as the Eightfold Path. It's regarded as a golden mean between self-indulgence and self-mortification, rejections of extremes. Aristotle's idea of the Golden Mean was similar. Moreover, taking things in stride, going with the flow and not trying to push the river in any relationship helps maintain it. Learning not to overreact to any situation as well as paying attention to what your partner considers important is paramount for the long- term success and happiness in it.

<u>Sunshine</u> is the necessary component for photosynthesis, which is how plants make food for themselves. Scientifically speaking, it's the process by which green plants use sunlight to synthesize foods

73

from carbon dioxide and water. Photosynthesis in plants involves the green pigment called chlorophyll which generates oxygen as a byproduct. My analogy for the sunshine needed in a relationship is belief and faith in ourselves and our partner, knowing that we will be there for each other.

If we genuinely care for the other's wellbeing and their commitment to our relationship, it is more likely to thrive. Letting our inner sunshine beam brightly with our love, devotion, dedication, and humor nourishes the unified whole. Knowing whatever our partner's specific love languages are will help keep our relationship fresh, long-standing, and rewarding.

Time and patience are required when we are looking for a relationship or healing after a bad break up.

Time is equally important to devote to one's relationship after it's established. Quality time, not looking at your cell phone when the other is talking. Not multitasking either. Paying attention when they are telling you something they deem important. When we do the things necessary to make our relationship work, we work on it, so it works for us. It will make yours stand the test of time. We can hope to mark many years together barring death.

Harvest Time- Oh, those sweet, heavenly rewards of our toil and labor, sumptuous, delicious fruits, crisp, tasty, healthy vegetables, abundant fragrant flowers, and fresh pungent herbs. Can't you just smell them now? The utter joy which a beautiful garden or yard can bring while it grows. The bonus is you helped create it, the pride you will feel just seeing its growth will be part of the payoff for your work. Like a loving relationship, its emotional fruits will be produced, felt, and enjoyed simply by doing the work. The returns are myriad, for example, how it makes you feel knowing you've got a great friend who has your back and loves you despite your flaws. Someone who will take care of you when you become sick. One who will listen to you and assure you everything is going to work out. Who knows exactly how you like to be kissed. That special person who wants the absolute best for you.

They know the happier you are with them, the better they in turn will endeavor to add to your relationship. You cannot put a monetary price on the incredible happiness you will experience when your ship comes in.

How have you prepared the soil in your life?

What seeds are you planting?

Are you tending the garden well?

CHAPTER 6:

OF COURSE, I CAN HANDLE THE TRUTH

"You are imperfect, permanently and inevitably flawed.
And you are beautiful."
~Amy Bloom

As mentioned in the last chapter, I needed to do a full assessment of myself to create a better version of myself, to align with my core being as it were; a more compassionate, less angry, less judgmental man.

I got an idea from one of my favorite movies, A Few Good Men.

Picture the scene where Tom Cruise is grilling Jack Nicholson's character in the courtroom. Nicholson barks back at Tom Cruise's character, "You can't handle the truth." It gave me pause and made me start to ponder my failed relationships and dating that went awry. Hmmm…could I handle the truth? I thought about if for a week or so then decided; yeah, I can handle it. I created a journal listing all the relationships I believed that I screwed up and even women I had dated a few times, to figure out what went wrong. Some things were obvious.

My ego thwarted many. That said, I reached out to past girlfriends whom I had remained friends with, or at least was their acquaintance. Some were amazed I remembered them; some were surprised I was able to find them. Others were wondering if I was truly serious when I told them I was attempting to change my wicked ways. (Humor seemed to break down any concerns that I was trying to date them again and put them at ease.) It also allowed me to apologize if apropos and close a festering emotional wound.

I told myself I wouldn't judge their answers no matter how difficult it was to hear. I also would see if I agreed with their assessment of my character.

Here's an abbreviated list of my high crimes and misdemeanors. No names mentioned.

One lady said I was too NEEDY, and she felt smothered. Yes, that was true, I have since become emotionally stronger and don't tend to smother people anymore. Spoil maybe...

One lady admitted she still smoked cigarettes; she knew that was a deal killer for me (More on Deal Killers in the next chapter) She initially told me she only occasionally had a smoke when she drank. She hid it quite well from me for a while.

One woman admitted that she used me to make her old boyfriend jealous. She thought I was too nice for her; she needed her BAD BOY back. She said she actually married him, and they were together for many years.

Hmmm... okay, I could accept that.

One told me I was way too intense for her. I was loud, obnoxious, and overly enthusiastic. Yes, I concur with that; I still am today. Perhaps not quite as intense. Luckily for me my wife hasn't killed me...yet...

One woman whom I was dating before I was married to my first wife told me she was upset that I fell asleep during our lovemaking. Unbelievably, it happened two times before she blew me off. She wrote me an understandingly nasty message in her lipstick on my bedroom mirror. What a complete LOSER and A' Hole I was. Yes, that was true, my only excuse was drinking too much champagne both times. I can laugh about it now however it hurt her feelings badly as I was, according to her, her first real love which I apologized for many years ago.

One said, "Tom, sorry to tell you but I think you're weird." Yes, guilty as charged. I am a different duck. My great friend Marc has been telling me for years "That I am not for everyone, but I am for him". I am an acquired taste after all. To be completely honest here, I have always been considered a little strange, asking out of the box questions, seeing things differently than many.

The crazy reaches I have when making a pun for example.

My friends would say, "Tom you're a very Punny guy. With a straight face, my facial expressions went into SERIOUS MODE: I would stare intensely, directly into their eyes and reply; "Let me understand this ...I'm Punny, how? You mean Punny, like I'm a clown? I amuse you? I make you laugh? I'm here to fricking amuse you? Whattya you mean Punny? Punny how? How am I so Punny?" Then I'd smile.

That said, this is my uniqueness. I will not, nor can I change the way my mind is wired. I LIKE ME. I like how my mind processes information. My true friends like me too.

One told me I was too short. She initially thought she could deal with that, but it started bugging her that she was taller. I said, true that, and it is one personal attribute I can't change. Luckily for me my wife is cool with towering over me. She thinks it empowers her.

One lady said she hated my little man syndrome, my bragging about my accomplishments, and my nasty one-upmanship which I would use to belittle people that I didn't care for. True again, of course, I did it to make myself feel better. I had low self-esteem in those days. I didn't correct her nor make excuses. She wished me well and said that she wished she knew the man I had grown up to become. I truly felt good after talking with her.

One woman refused to talk on the phone, instead, she emailed me and said she didn't want to chat. The reason she dropped me like a hot potato (her vernacular) was my narcissism. Now that one hurt, probably because it was true. Again, my ego was trampled by low self-esteem.

There was a blessing in her words. Since it hurt me, it meant subconsciously I knew I still had work to do. A huge emotional weight had been lifted by accepting and moving on.

One lady who I was truly smitten with said it wasn't me, it was merely timing. She had just ended an LTR and wasn't done grieving. She had put herself on

MATCH.COM too early and apologized that she hadn't been truthful. She's since remarried and has three lovely boys.

One lady said I was too Liberal for her as she was a staunch Republican and knew she didn't want to be with someone of my political perspective. I wore that title with honor like my Battle E medal from my Navy days. Yes, I'm a Liberal and proud of it.

The last one I will share here is the long-distance relationship which I had shortly after I divorced. I met her on an online dating site. It lasted primarily via text messages and long phone calls for many months. She was beautiful and funny.

We finally met in Disneyworld in Florida, somewhere she had always wanted to visit. My imagination was too powerful because when we physically met, she wasn't what I expected. I could deal with that. We continued dating, then I flew to her state and spent the weekend with her. She had a tumultuous 5-year-old boy who I couldn't stand. I hemmed and hawed about it and figured since I loved this woman, I would be the bigger man. Sadly, I didn't contain my anger towards that little brat. When I returned home from our short visit, she ended it.

Again, it was the right call. I wasn't a great father by any means in the first place and probably would have made the kid miserable with my authoritarian ways. I already knew why this one failed and didn't need to hear it from her. Also, I was on the rebound. I hadn't been dating that long. It was exciting connecting with someone who made me feel like a King. Sadly, I wasn't aware at the time that I had fallen in "Love with LOVE", not the person. Since learning about that concept I have heard many stories of other "Hopeless Romantics" who also have succumbed to this issue.

It took many months to come to grips with what happened. Many were indeed my issues, some were not. Age has given me the gift of knowing what issues I could change, which ones I could not and the wisdom to know the difference between them.

I will end this chapter with a Blog posting I wrote on "Falling in Love with Love"

Oh, man, if only I could have learned this simple, but profound lesson early on in my lonely single life. Looking back today with more mature eyes, having become more emotionally grounded, I lament just how many beautiful relationships could have blossomed. Sadly, they never did. I tried too hard to impress, gave too much too soon, shared way too much too early on… the bottom line was that I wanted to make it work so badly.

I got so excited believing I finally found "The One" that I acted impulsively without thinking of the other; they had become my object of desire. So I smothered, acted controlling, and ended up pushing these class act women away. That putrid stench of neediness permeated my being.

Sadly, I allowed this to happen to me more than once. Being blinded by lovesickness is no fun. It took over my rational brain and put me on an endless emotional roller coaster of unfilled, unquenchable desire.

The truth was that I fell in love with the "idea of love," got swept up in its alluring euphoria and not the real person. This works both ways in any romantic relationship.

My biggest mistake with regard to the long-distance relationship I just shared was I created an image in my mind which in no way matched the real person.

This is still something I occasionally struggle with today; there is a fine line between being a man wanting to show his partner how much he cares and coming off too intense and having to be with her every second and never giving her enough space to breathe.

I feel blessed to have finally become aware of my "glomming on" aspect of my persona. I have married someone who helps keep me on an emotional even keel. Just that one look and Michelle immediately helps me to see the bigger picture. Truth be told, I almost lost this one too. For the first time in my adult life, I let my ego go. I didn't try to impress her as I once would have. Talk is cheap. Actions show one's real character. It's worked wonders for me. Anyone can learn from my myriad mistakes. If you are not willing to see yourself in an unflattering light, you will never grow to your full potential.

I assure you that if I can do this, anyone can. Don't give up. Allow things to unfold naturally. It does no good to push the river. Keep the faith. I'm a believer that we receive the love we believe we are worthy of. Don't overlook a potentially rewarding relationship because on the surface it doesn't seem like the "Perfect One".

Follow your heart, trust your gut, but take your mind with you.

If you took inventory and considered all of the relationships you have been in, what would you learn about yourself?

If you didn't like what you realized, what could you do to compensate?

Are there people from your past with whom you need to make amends?

CHAPTER 7:

TO STAY OR NOT TO STAY, THAT IS THE QUESTION

"The opposite of love is not hate,
it's indifference. The opposite of art is not ugliness,
it's indifference. The opposite of faith is not heresy,
it's indifference. And the opposite of life is not death,
it's indifference."
~Elie Wiesel

Deal killers

We all have things that we won't tolerate in our relationships. I knew the things I was looking for in my quest to creating my dream relationship. What I needed to do was formulate lists, as this method works best for me.

I compiled two separate ones and the headings read:

What was I looking for?

What would I not tolerate?

Here's my "D.O.A." list

Smoking cigarettes, not even when she has a drink or is upset

Hatred

Abuse of any kind

Manipulation of any kind

Meanness

Bitchiness

Lying

Infidelity

Indifference/Emotional coldness

Controlling

Guilt tripping

Game playing

Religious zealots

Non-Gratefulness

Anger issues

Perpetual Gas lighter

University of Washington Football Fan, just kidding.

These sprung to the top of my mind. I had to make damn sure I didn't have those issues if I expected my future wife to respect me. I wondered what things others considered "deal breakers." As mentioned, from time to time during my ongoing research on this project, I would pose questions to the group.

You've seen my Relationship Killers, here's what the group said.

The question was:

"What things are Deal Killers for you in romantic relationships?"

Here's what they wrote:

Substance Abuse

Alcohol Abuse

Domestic Abuse

Mental Abuse

Emotional Abuse

Verbal Abuse

Sexual Abuse

Anger issues

Overly Needy

Jealousy

Violence

Treated as a Doormat

Hypocrisy

Cheating/Infidelity (This one had the greatest number of votes)

Intolerance

Meanness

Disrespect

Disloyalty

Dishonesty

Lying

Stealing

Racism

Narcissism

Neglect

Hostility

Indifference/Aloofness

Emotional Coldness

Insulting

Hatred

Controlling

Humiliation

Criticizing

Negating

Negative Attitude

Shaming

Accusing

Blaming

Denial

Using Guilt

Game Playing

Withholding Affection

Codependency

Manipulation- physical or emotional

Ultimatums

Bullying

Detachment

Gambling

Gossip

Passive Aggressiveness

Perfectionism

Brow Beating

Negative Attitudes

Condescending

Character assassination

Vindictiveness

Constant Complaining and Whining~ aka bellyaching, crybaby, grumbling, moaning, sniveling, squawking, kvetching, peevishness

Moodiness

Belligerence

Haughtiness

Arrogance

Icy Coldness

Scolding

Selfishness

Ignoring Boundaries

Possessiveness

Unreliability

Pettiness

Cruelty

Vengefulness

Irresponsibility

Inconsistency

Rage

Game Playing

Disrespectful

Racism/Fanaticism

Apathy

Gaslighting…While I didn't elaborate on any of the aforementioned offenses, I did want to shed light on this important one.

Wikipedia states: "Gaslighting is a form of psychological manipulation in which a person or a group covertly sows seeds of doubt in a targeted individual, making them question their memory, perception, or judgment, often evoking in them cognitive dissonance and other changes such as low self-esteem."

Oxford Dictionary states: "Manipulate (someone) by psychological means into questioning their sanity."

What are your non-negotiables?

Have you settled for less than what you deserve or desire rather than be alone?

Are you willing to boldly state what you want and don't want?

Respect Romance Honesty
Happiness Kindness Admiration Laughter
Compassion Chemistry Empathy Commitment
Sharing Openness Transparency Patience
Dependability Equality Partnership Selflessness
Interdependence Understanding Authenticity
Passion Companionship Autonomy

Love   Trust
Generosity
Friendship
Communication
Forgiveness

CHAPTER 8:

NEEDS, WE ALL HAVE 'EM

"The meeting of two personalities is like the contact of
two chemical substances:
if there is any reaction,
both are transformed."
~ Carl Jung

In continuation of my deep examination and assessment of what I wanted in my next relationship I wrote down some of what I considered to be critical for me. I wasn't going to be shy or sugarcoat it, nor was I holding anything back. Knowing the difference between my wants vs. needs made this easier to create.

My list follows:

Communication

Compassion

Humor

Mutual Respect

Honesty

Commitment

Spiritualty

Passion

Sexual Compatibility

Kindness

Forgiveness

Happiness

Friendship

Harmonious Relations

Love of Cats

And Trust.

As mentioned, I was seeking others' opinions when writing this book. I threw the following question to my focus group.

"Please leave one word… What is the most important aspect of your relationship? Or one you desire above all else." The following are the responses.

The top five mentioned had the most similar answers from the group.

Trust

Communication

Truth

Friendship

Honesty

Commitment

Mutual Exclusiveness

Laughter

Giving

Mutual Respect

Happiness

Kindness

Compassion

Chemistry

Empathy

Perseverance

Forgiveness

Connection

God/Creator

Reciprocity

Sweetness

Openness

Transparency

Self-Worth

Tolerance

Spiritual Commonality

Patience

Protection

Dependability

Reliability

Devoutness

Loyalty

Partnership

Humility

Congruence

Selflessness

Peace

Grace

Depth

Closeness

Synchronicity

Intent

Resilience

Commonality

Physical Touch

Authenticity

Forever Minded

Companionship

Passion

Helpfulness

Oneness

Purity

Equality

Listening

Belief

Hope

Affection

Unconditional

Fun

Direct Eye Contact

Transparency

And Autonomy.

I want to give special attention to Autonomy as it was one I hadn't fully considered adding until a wise former therapist brought it up. I researched it and felt it worthy of additional mention. The following information was derived from several sources. I found it refreshing!

Au·ton·o·my

Apart from the need for relatedness, the need for autonomy, and the need for competence also play a major role in relationship satisfaction. If within the relationship the need for autonomy is fulfilled, this predicts higher relationship satisfaction, more commitment to the relationship, and fewer conflicts.

It turns out that how one love partner experiences the fulfillment of their need for autonomy not only predicts how satisfied that person is but also predicts how satisfied their partner is.

Autonomy is not the same as independence, avoidance of intimacy, lack of interest, and care or rebellion. Instead, autonomy is a deeply felt personal endorsement for your actions and your commitment to other people. You could see it as the difference between reactive autonomy and reflective autonomy.

Autonomy comes from ancient Greek roots meaning "self" and nomos meaning "custom" or "law." This reflects the political sense of the word — a group's right to self-government or self-rule. When a person seeks autonomy, he or she would like to be able to make decisions independently from an authority figure.

Can you relate?

The capacity of an agent to act in accordance with objective morality rather than under the influence of desires.

In developmental psychology and moral, political, and bioethical philosophy, autonomy is the capacity to make an informed, uncoerced decision.

Autonomy is a person's need to perceive that they have choices, that what they are doing is of their own volition, and that they are the source of their actions. The way managers and leaders frame information and situations either promote the likelihood that a person will perceive autonomy or undermines it.

In closing, I found everyone's comments and preferences heartfelt yet uniquely personal to them.

It made me ponder just how alike we all are and yet have different wants, needs, and desires. Knowing our wants and our those of our partners makes it possible to create a long-lasting relationship. This point is well documented by Dr. Gary Chapman. His classic book *The 5 Love Languages, the Secret to Love that Lasts* had a profound effect on my life as well as that of millions (literally) of other people worldwide. In a nutshell, he puts love into 5 major categories.

They are as follows: Words of Affirmation, Acts of Service, Receiving Gifts, Quality Time, and Physical Touch. Each one is important and expresses love in its special way. Learning your partner's and your primary love language will help create a stronger bond in your relationship. In the same way, knowing your partner's core values wants, needs, and desires helps a couple keep their relationship strong and long-lasting. I highly recommend his bestselling book. It changed my life.

What do you value in relationships?

What are your love languages in order?

In what ways do you claim your autonomy?

CHAPTER 9:

OPINIONS, EVERYBODY'S GOT ONE

"The goal is to laugh forever with someone you take seriously.
~ Maya Angelou

I had been doing my due diligence for a year; reading books, watching TED Talks, and listening to books on CD. I had done my assessments of what I was looking for, and what I wouldn't tolerate. Still it felt as though something was missing. I wasn't per se looking to hit the Psychologist's couch again (I had done that dance for several years during my first marriage). I was simply looking for helpful suggestion on what advice people found valuable.

As previously mentioned, in the course of researching this book, I would occasionally throw out questions to the group. Here's a recent one below, no judgment on my part. Take what you like and discard what doesn't resonate with you. You win by knowing your mind and the things you hold dear. I found the following comments quite telling and beneficial to consider.

My question was: "If you were giving relationship advice to a friend, What is the most important thing you would mention?"

The following are some of the answers/suggestions they offered.

"Listen to understand, not to respond."

"Be your authentic self. If the other person doesn't respond in kind with love and respect, then they are not the one for you."

"Don't be so brittle to not be open to a new love. Give people a chance. Don't look for reasons to give up."

"Total communication right from start!!!"

"Integrity, forgiveness, avoiding gratuitous drama at all costs."

"Real kindness seeks no return."

"Be confident in yourself!! Allow your partner to do the same."

"Remember to have respect and humor."

"Empathy: Understanding that your partner is perhaps just as vulnerable, misunderstood, needy, emotional, and as wanting as you are — they may just express and desire differently."

"Listen to your own counsel."

"Put your significant other's needs first in everything you think and do. If both of you do this and act on the other needs everything will fall into place."

"Integrity and honesty."

"Don't do anything to someone that you wouldn't want to be done to you."

"I'd rather be hurt by the truth than to find out I'd been lied to!"

"Trust is so important. It is essential to be able to communicate that you can feel secure and safe in your relationship."

"Say thank you for all things big and small. Even if my beautiful wife just warms up a cup of noodles I am genuinely thankful, so I tell her. Her smile lights up the whole room and remember to be thankful. ALWAYS! "

"I would advise them not to take any one-size-fits-all advice."

"Remember that you are worthy of the partner you truly desire, so choose wisely."

"Be honest, you instill trust into your relationship that way."

"Can't speak for other couples; but the foundation of our marriage is our mutual belief in the deity and sanctity of God. You have to be on the same page for things to work in the long run."

"While I'm not an expert, I had advice from a long-time married friend I loved. He shared have words that matter. For them using the words "it is important to me that..." means drop everything and do it unless it is life or death on your side. He added that he hoped the other word was true in other relationships "I promise" means at all cost and integrity." I loved this!

"Many great pieces of lasting relationship and marriage advice can be distilled down to a few simple words: Love is a choice, not a feeling. I added, For me, Love is a feeling...we choose whether or not to align with it."

"Above all be best friends as well as lovers. Lust will end, the friendship will endure."

"Trust your gut. Follow your heart but take your brain with you."

"Stay with it since it may get hard. Very effing hard - but recall what brought you together and remember your vows. It gets a hell of a lot better when you emerge on the other side."

"Remember that real love is not supposed to have conditions. You don't get to pick and choose the moments you want to love another human being. Real love is accepting the person the way they are despite their bad moments, while at the same time encouraging them to continue to learn and grow. When you let your expectations in a relationship become ultimatums; you are forgetting that unconditional love doesn't have requirements. To genuinely love another human being, you have to first accept them as they are now, not their potential. In relationships, true acceptance is the only way I know how to love someone. It's a ridiculously hard thing to do."

"Be truly healed and love yourself enough to act out of inspiration with open eyes when getting involved with another romantically and take your time. There is no rush. Only fools rush in."

"There are worse things than being single, like being in the wrong relationship."

"Unless their behavior causes emotional or physical harm, engage softly, validate the other's feelings. Ask your partner what resolution they'd like? Try to reach a compromise. Then shut your mouth and mentally move ON."

"Compromise is a good last resort; however, I prefer creative problem-solving."

"Do not react - listen, acknowledge, and mentally digest and return with carefully thought out response/resolution in the best interest of the relationship not the individuals."

"I'd ask them to be honest and think about what quality in a mate is most important for them. And do they possess it too?"

"Be radically honest and specific from the get-go; at worst, it will shorten a doomed relationship in which compatibility likely would have been an issue."

"Love, honor, respect, and compromise!"

"If you pick a mate based on the fact that they are just like you, you might as well just pick YOU. Even a magnet knows, opposites attract."

"Keep your own identity, your own friends, interests, hobbies, etc. Don't be joined at the hip. You may be "one" in a sense, but you still need to be "you". I've seen too many couples (especially young ones in a new relationship), living in each other's pockets. They ditch their friends and spend every waking minute together. It rarely lasts. Controlling partners generally want you to let go of everything that makes you, you. That's a big red flag."

"My advice is to look for those opportunities; to encourage and uplift the one you love, using the warmth and tenderness of an unexpected hug. Or the comfort of soothing words of love that come directly from your heart. If one does what is expected; the one you love, will know nothing different. But the person who does the unexpected, it can certainly bring a pleasant surprise that will excite and stir feelings of joy and happiness in the love of your life."

"You must first like your own company before you are ready to be in a relationship."

"Respect each other; if you lose respect, you are not good for each other."

"Unpack your OWN baggage and deal with it first vs. pushing the blame/focus on others."

"Friendship is the most important aspect of any romantic relationship, and honesty."

"Accept and appreciate the person for who they are."

"You be you". Be the beautiful, radiant, loving you first. Be whole."

"Be your own best friend."

"Communicate from your heart."

"Pick your fights. Come on it is not all roses and pansies. Know what is really important, you'll find not much is!"

"Communication- Get rid of the ego; have the best intentions for your partner and assume your partner does as well. Create a safe space for each other."

"Listen and speak with love and honesty."

"Know yourself and love yourself deeply before you seek relation with another. When you are in a relationship, or beginning one, find ways to be together and ways to be alone. Support yours and your Beloved's highest good."

"The wisdom of Eeyore provides me a reminder "Silly of me I know, but we all have our little ways." Always allow for each other's little ways."

"Be open, honest, and transparent."

"Talk about it as it comes up. Don't put things in an emotional backpack to dump later."

"Date nights."

"Communicate to understand more than to make sure your point is understood."

"Be gentle with yourself and your partner."

"Know and love yourself first, then all will be well."

"Understand that humans are singular beings, and to check your ego and insecurities before you look to point a finger at any partner."

"We don't own anyone's time, emotions, or body. The sooner we are willing to learn accept and apply this, the healthier and better relationships we can have."

"Let go of past hurts. Just because one partner did something hurtful doesn't mean that your new partner is doing the same thing."

"Be yourself."

"Don't give yourself away. Hold true to yourself, your values, your commitments. Love makes it easy to lose sight of that stuff. It focuses you entirely outward. Don't forget to keep your locus of control internal."

"Took me years to understand that very few of us are easy to live with. Most of us suffer from something, generally something no one knows about, we fight inner battles, etc. Important to remember, when we meet someone who is willing to be a part of your life, commits to understanding you, wants to grow with you, knows your shortcomings and accepts you as you are, work hard to keep that one."

"Great loves don't come along that often. Be ready, open, and aware when they do. Sometimes we let a great one slip away only realizing that when it's too late."

"Don't let pride, ego, or perfectionism ruin a real relationship."

"Far better to choose happiness over being right."

"Always take your partner into consideration, when making choices, and major decisions. Establish ground rules for your relationship, learn what your partner needs to feel loved."

"Knowing yourself allows you to know the other – this allows a couple to have a soul connection and really "know" each other."

"No one can complete your life, but you do share your life with someone."

"What one feels, they radiate, what they radiate, they attract."

"Choose each other every day. Find ways to make sure your partner feels loved and supported every day. You have to be in this together and be there for each other."

I found this posting to be a big hit on my Facebook page. Lots of good, useful information methinks. It showed me that I had a long way to go to find "The One"

However I was learning many things about myself which were invaluable.

Master through the ebbs and flows. There are times when you want to be right next to that person, touching and you know.. he he...there are also times when you just want them to be away. Get through those times and be easy with each other and you can always find your way back to who you are as a couple.

People change through the years/decades and you have to allow that change and fit back together in a different way. Again, being easy on each other. With your hearts, your mind and even your bodies.

Another friend offered his relationship wisdom, "Jean and I had a tough beginning. My Mom died the week we were to be married. We buried her in the dress she made for the wedding. 30 days later we got married. Commitment is the key! When you take an oath to God you better keep it. You can fall out of love, but it is your commitment to God that makes you love again. My CPA said: "I know how to double your money, STAY MARRIED!"

One of the pillars of all healthy relationships is good communication. Once that is gone, so follows everything else. I've found reflective listening is a great tool to use. Simply by restating what you believe you have heard from the other not only lets them know you are interested in understanding them, it removes any vagueness and clarifies their point. The more this is done, the deeper the relationship develops.

I love the following quote from *Men are from Mars, Women are from Venus* by John Gray: "When a man can listen to a woman's feeling without getting angry and frustrated, he gives her a wonderful gift. He makes her feel safe."

Quit trying to change your partner. If you need to change them perhaps you made the wrong decision initially to pursue them. Certain behaviors that drive you crazy can be addressed such as hygiene habits, mannerism, unorganized living, etc. Just my thought but if their core being is bothering you, a life change may be in order; only you can know that for sure.

No relationships are perfect; they work because people are willing to work on them daily. They care enough for the other to move through the rough patches. When they find the issues, they develop ways to deal with them. Both parties have a desire to make them work.

My great friend, Portland musician and philosopher Tom Civiletti reminds us that recognizing our emotional states has a great ability to help us be as we want to be. If we feel anger, jealousy, fear, or shame, observing that emotion within us gives us the power not to be ruled by that emotion.

I love this quote by Eleanor Brown, "Rest and self-care are so important. When you take time to replenish your spirit, it allows you to serve others from the overflow. You cannot serve from an empty vessel."

What advice would you offer that has helped you in engaging in relationship?

What has worked?

What hasn't worked?

CHAPTER 10:

SEEK AND YE SHALL FIND

"I've finally found The One.
He dwells in my own Heart"
~ Thomas E. Ziemann

I've always loved that biblical quote, Matthew 7 Verse 7 since it shares deep wisdom. For me, it meant if I knew exactly what I was looking for, in this case "The One" I would stand a great chance of meeting her. While I had been out of the dating scene for many years, I had done good work internally on myself. Now came the practical application. At least I finally figured out that to attract the person or relationship my heart had been pining for, I needed to be attractive. I'm not talking about physical looks. I'm suggesting the inner magnetism we all have. We call to us what we are.

Compassion, self-love, kindness, and honesty barely scratches the surface. Become the person you desire and watch what beauty unfolds in your life.

It became abundantly clear that I needed to become my own Soulmate. So many people search endlessly for "The One/The All", never looking inward to experience their own ineffable beauty that exists beyond their emotions and mind. By becoming my own best friend, accepting all my good qualities as well as my faults helped me to heal old wounds. It allows greater opportunities to bring that relationship I've always sought. Knowing the difference between being alone and lonely is paramount here. For many years, I have followed the adage, "It's far better to be alone than to wish I was". I have chosen never to settle for mediocrity. Ms. Right Now over Ms. Right for me. For me, keeping a positive attitude, an open heart, and belief that the woman of my dreams simply hadn't materialized yet had helped keep my heart in the game. Generally, I found it's simply timing or geography that had stymied what I was looking for. What I did was forget about finding the perfect mate. If you're seeking inner peace and a long-lasting meaningful life partnership, give up seeking the "Perfect Partner," seek rather one who's perfect for you. Perfection in people has never existed.

You will attain greater inner peace by searching for the one who accepts fully, your inner beauty, and your flaws equally.

So many people reject an amazing person believing that an even better one is out there, rarely taking the time to fully discover the beauty in their mate or even knowing fully what they genuinely want.

Here are some of the ways I came up with to find her.

I put myself out there- Time to put the pedal to the metal so to speak. I started letting everyone know I was single and looking. You'd be surprised how many people had suggestions or knew of a single lady. A critical point there is always to follow up on their lead. Be sure to thank them! Your friends were kind enough to try and play matchmaker, so don't be a flake. In case it doesn't work out with the one they suggested; they will try again if they know you were seriously looking. Try to get as much information about the other person to see if there's commonality.

Suggest an email before calling them. If they seem like a possibility, offer them your phone number or you'd be happy to call them. If the phone call(s) go well, meet them for coffee or some other casual interaction. Find a place with people around, where you both can feel comfortable. Word to the wise is NOT to drink any alcohol at your meeting. Keep a clear head, save the wine until you have a real dinner date. You can also determine the role alcohol plays in that person's life, since they may not drink at all or you may discover that the two of you may have different consumption styles and comfort levels around alcohol. You will want to put on your best Date Face so there will be another if that's your goal.

Whether it goes well, or you don't care to date the person again, be courteous. You know how it feels to get hurt. Simply say that you enjoyed your time and thank them for meeting you. Be honest but kind. I would say, I would enjoy keeping your friendship, but I am not ready to commit at this time. It's a difficult thing to do, but necessary so they don't get their hopes up if you don't see a future together.

Dating Services- I am a firm believer in this way to meet people. Word to the wise- use a recent photo, nothing worse than finally meeting a person you've had correspondence with, and they look nothing like the photo in their profile. They used an outdated photo or heaven forbid not even theirs, to begin with. Bad Juju!

Make sure that your profile is well-written without any grammatical errors. If you are lacking in that department, hit up one of your writer friends to help you create one. Do it from the heart.

Don't make the mistake of copying someone else's profile and using it as your own since the person you are trying to attract can usually guess you didn't write it. You lose immediate credibility that way.

Churches/Synagogue/Place of Worship- If religion is your thing, those places are a great locations to mingle and meet people of your spiritual mindset.

Make yourself available- Now that you've committed to finding your mate, make the time to put yourself out there, even when you don't feel like it. It takes some work and daily effort if you really want to make it happen. Don't use the excuse that you're too tired and then complain that you can't find anyone. Follow up on those social network texts and dating site profiles. When prospecting for gold, one rarely hits the mother lode without effort. Put yourself in places where likeminded people congregate. Strike up small talk with them to see if there's any spark. If there is, plan to meet up. Speaking of Meet Ups, they are another great way to connect with people while doing things that interest you. Google local Meet Ups in your area, create the profile of your likes and interests, this is FREE to do. Sign up for what you like and GO!

Here are some ideas:

Social Settings

The grocery store

The Zoo

Aquarium

Wineries

Chili Cook-Offs

Farmers markets

Festivals of any kind

Happy hours in restaurants

If you're in school, on campus is a perfect place to meet folks

Forest and hiking trails

The beach/coast

Museums

Parties that your friends are hosting are particularly good

Parks

Forest Preserves

Nature Trails

Concerts/Plays/Live performances

Volunteer groups

Charity functions

Flea markets/Rummage sales/Garage sales

Silent and Live Auctions

Book Signings

Speed Dating, (Hey, don't knock it til' you try it)

The sky's the limit; have some fun deciding what floats your boat but do it. Be PROACTIVE!

Now with every endeavor, there is the risk of rejection. Follow your dreams anyway. This is a numbers game. Timing also plays a part. Be open to the possibilities that await you. If you are turned down, pick yourself back up and get back on the horse. It took Edison literally 10,000 attempts to find the carbon filament for his lightbulb. He endured much ridicule along the way from the press and other scientists saying he was a failure and he'd never figure it out. Thankfully for all of us he never gave up.

Quit wishing for your dream love and pursue it. The universe prefers the backbone over the wishbone.

What methods have you used to meet potential partners?

What are some of your interests that might have you cross paths with them?

Are you willing to try something new?

Chapter 11:

If You're Happy and You're Single, Clap Your Hands

"The first lesson of love
is to learn how to be alone."
~Osho

Having spent many years being single, I can honestly say that while it was lonely at times, it was necessary to get my inner house in order. This time not only allowed me to become comfortable with my own company and newly created persona, but it also permitted me to take a deeper look at myself; to really assess and fully accept my strengths, weaknesses, personality flaws, quirks, and idiosyncrasies without judgment, excuses or lamentations.

Being willing to see myself in an unflattering light did several things for me. Once I was able to acknowledge what I didn't like about myself and not hating who I had become, it allowed me to accept my shortcomings and work diligently to overcome them. Once mastered, I didn't have to relearn the mistake which caused needless unhappiness, breakups, and lost friendships.

To get to LIKE myself, really love myself was a huge obstacle. I find this same issue when I go out and speak to audiences. I pose the question: "At this very second, who do you love more than anyone else in the world?" At that point, the room becomes quiet. I will ask again; do you love yourself MORE than anyone else in your life? Sadly, very few can unequivocally say that they could.

I believe no book on relationships would be complete without a nod to "Singlehood". Many years of empirical research and lengthy discussions with many relationship experts, therapists have opened my eyes to a few thoughts I will share.

Being single is usually a choice with a myriad of reasons behind it. Sometimes a person has been so emotionally ravaged and devastated from the loss or being hurt by someone who they loved that they will never allow that to happen again. Their motto is: "Far better to be alone than be hurt again." I liken this to a person who loses a cherished pet; it was that one in a million connection that the grief they suffered was far too great to have to endure again. This can be especially true of the death of a spouse. Their grief never went away. Some will carry this cross to their graves perhaps wearing it as a badge of commitment or to honor their deceased partner.

Sometimes a person is afraid of commitment, not wanting to repeat dysfunctional patterns. They may want to keep their options open to see if someone better comes along. Other times it may be a person's negative attitude and actions that thwart their relationship early on and it never gets a chance to blossom.

People have shared they won't settle for just any relationship and are incredibly discerning and discriminating which I applaud. They have the belief that, they are not single, they simply aren't taken. They are on reserve for someone who deserves their heart. They might also be of the mindset they are strong enough to be alone, live life to its fullest and never have to depend on others. These people have set boundaries and have high expectations and standards.

Online folks have told me they didn't believe they were worthy of a quality relationship. As the adage goes "We generally receive the love we believe we are deserving of."

In some cases, nose to the grindstone, hardworking business executives have placed their careers above everything else. Many times their health also suffers as a direct result. They are fulfilled by their work.

A sad point to remember is that many marriages fail due to one partner not doing that daily work a healthy, loving relationship requires. In their mind, they are the breadwinners trying to help their family and their spouse should realize their sacrifice they are making working 70 hours a week. Hard for me to fathom what good the money is if you exchange your relationship for it. Many end up divorced, losing much of the wealth they worked so hard to attain.

Some people are jaded and choose to remain single. When you ask them what happened, they will give you many reasons; they are tired of giving the other the world and receiving nothing in return, or their ex was cruel, they cheated on them, they didn't know how to communicate, and when they focused on someone they showed them why they needed to be alone. I never argue with them as their reasons are right for them.

They hold these three adages deep within their psyches.

Far better to be alone, than to wish you were.

Far better to be alone than to hate yourself for staying in an abusive relationship.

Far better to be alone than allowing your partner to destroy your inner peace.

Some people stay single because of personal illness, and don't want to put that burden on a potential partner.

Some have many fears, fears of fully committing, fears they will have to deal with everything that comes with a relationship as well as the compromises they fear they will have to make.

Some never had time for a relationship; I am reminded of Billy Joel's classic lyrics: "Now Paul is a real estate novelist, who never had time for a wife." He was talking to Davey who most likely was single too, lol.

Some men are all about the conquest and the physical aspects. They have no interest in a relationship and would prefer hanging out with the boys.

Then there's the Happily Single crowd, they enjoy their own company and don't like the idea of anyone they need to be accountable to. They love their freedom. They don't care what others think, they like being alone.

I am all about having that kind of relationship with myself. Being one's bestie is the greatest gift we can give ourselves.

There are some who lack the emotional maturity to keep a relationship; it's always the fault of the other that it didn't work out.

I remember like this like it was yesterday. I got some great advice when I was single from a phenomenally successful businesswoman whom I had known for years said, "Tom, quit looking for Ms. Right. Now is the time for you to rebuild your life. Finish those books you've told me about, write down your goals and work to achieve them. By doing so you become the Mr. Right for the woman of your dreams." I loved that.

On the flip side I found it comical that people would try to give me relationship advice on finding the one, yet they were still single.

I know a few people who most likely will never find what they are looking for because they are too picky, don't give people a chance, are seeking perfection. Truth is that there are no perfect relationships; the trick is finding one that's perfect for you.

There is no judgment here; no right or wrong, everyone must choose their path. Both singlehood and committed relationships have pluses and minuses, It's up to you to decide what's right for you. Word to the wise is

Creating the Relationship of Your Dreams

that it is far better to wait for Mr. Right then settle for Mr. Right now.

I will close this chapter the way it began, with a quote from one of my favorite mystics.

> "If you are not capable of being alone,
> your relationship is false. It's just a trick
> to avoid loneliness, nothing else."
> ~ Osho

What are some of the benefits of being a solo act?

Would you rather be alone for the right reasons than with someone for the wrong reasons?

Can you reframe the word alone to all-one?

As mentioned in the Introduction, this book would get a boost from two of the most knowledgeable women I know in the Relationship Industry.

Meet my friend Edie Weinstein. Internationally known bestselling book Author, Columnist, and Speaker. She's a Licensed Social Worker and graduate of the New Seminary in New York City, where she was ordained as an Interfaith Minister. Ms. Weinstein brings well over 40 years of experience to the table and has played an integral part in this book and my last one, *Taming the Anger Dragon, From Pissed off to Peaceful.* Edie's discerning "Velvet Pen" will help to smooth out the rough edges; plus add her vast wisdom to this project. A bonus is that she's got one of the biggest, most loving hearts on the planet!!

Chapter 12:

At 61, I Am Coming To Terms With The Possibility That I Will Remain Single-
~ Edie Weinstein

"A busy, vibrant, goal-oriented woman is so much more attractive than a woman who waits around for a man to validate her existence."
~ Mandy Hale

When I walked down the aisle on May 2, 1987, to share, the words "I do." with the man I had met seven months earlier, I anticipated that we would be spending a long lifetime together.

We had met when I was 28 and he was 36, introduced by a mutual friend during the intermission of a lecture by spiritual leader Ram Dass. Our marriage would be what I call "paradoxical," with its share of love and its own major dysfunctions that I shudder to think I allowed for the time we were together.

He grew up in a family with an alcoholic-rageaholic father, and a mother with depression and anxiety. His parents divorced and not amicably. He was expected to take sides.

The dynamic in my marriage fell into the category of chosen allegiances. If I wasn't "siding" with my husband against anyone who disagreed with him, I was not being loyal. I felt as if I was always being tested and found wanting.

I thought I could heal the emotional wounds that he carried, but I realized that it needed to be an inside job. His pain spilled over into our home.

In my marriage, love and abuse lay side by side. It was primarily emotional, with two incidents that were physical. Both times he expressed remorse, but I wondered when it might happen again. I was embarrassed to be in such a situation, since as a therapist I would have advised clients to leave.

In 1992, he was diagnosed with Hepatitis C and I became his caregiver, citing the "in sickness and health" part of our marriage vows. My hope was that as a result of his needing my assistance with his ADLs (activities of daily living), he would magically become kinder and more patient. That same year we adopted our son, then 5.

What I discovered, to my disappointment, was that even with my mad skills as a professional therapist, I was at a loss to facilitate a healthy relationship between Michael and myself. A month after we adopted him, I had an ectopic pregnancy. A few months after that, we lost our home to the raging winds and rising waters of Hurricane Andrew in Homestead, Florida. It could have heralded the end of the marriage, but we pulled together.

Michael took his last breath on Dec. 21,1998, and since then I have had short-term relationships, lovers, and friends with benefits. I have not been in a committed relationship since my husband died nearly 22 years ago. I call myself "incidentally poly," since it is not my consciously chosen lifestyle, but I have had several simultaneous connections.

I have done the internet dating thing off and on for years, being both delighted and disappointed. I had a catfishing experience a year or so ago, and I met one man who became a pivotal person in my life, but we knew we weren't soulmate material. We talk a few times a year now.

My son has told me that I will never find a man with the qualities I am looking for and that I need to be with a woman. I tell him that I haven't even met a woman I could see myself with, although I would welcome her if she does arrive.

I have another long-divorced friend who says it would take someone exceptional to take her out of her single life. While I love being single with the freedom to create my own life, I simultaneously miss the companionship of a partner. I have amazing friends who meet some of my needs. I wish I could create a composite person comprised of all the wonderful qualities of those I know.

I have done all the things relationship coaches advise, such as feng shui-ing my home, designing a vision board, making "the list" of qualities I desire in a partner, cleaning out a dresser drawer, acting as I would if I were in a relationship, journaling about it, being the kind of person I want to attract, loving myself as I want to be loved.

I have held wedding ceremonies in which I have "married" myself. I take myself on dates. I have no fear of going anywhere alone. Movies, dinner, concerts, walks in the park — all things I would love to do while holding hands with a significant other. I have written cards and poems to give to this person.

I have wistfully gazed at couples who are all mushy-gushy with each other and desire that. I have also heard stories about the vitriol and violence in relationships and sigh with relief that I am a party of one. It is so much less complicated when I am the only one who needs to make decisions that affect my life, the only one to get out the door on time, the only one whose cleanliness standards I meet, without expectations of someone else meeting mine.

When I officiate at a wedding as an interfaith minister or attend one as a guest, without a "plus one" at my side or on the dance floor, a sense of wistfulness overcomes me at times. I toggle back and forth on the daily.

I have worked with a few coaches who have assisted me in peeling off the layers and getting to know myself better but have not yet attracted the love of my life.

I used to believe that in order to be in love, people had to carry little baggage (or at least have it fit in the overhead compartment), have financial independence, be healthy and low maintenance with minimal drama, have it all sewn up in a nice, neat little package. Yet there are folks like me who have done the work to be relationship-ready, and who are still a solo act. And there are those who meet few or none of the criteria listed above who have devoted partners.

I know I am the real deal, the whole package, good relationship material, despite my wounds and fears of attracting the same dynamics as the undesirable ones in my marriage. Friends attempt to assure me that I won't, since I have grown dramatically in the two decades since Michael died.

A part of me died that day, too. The part that was, as he so eloquently put it, "an emotional contortionist who would bend over backward to please people, a deer caught in the headlights when it came to making a decision and was always looking over my shoulder to see if the propriety police were watching." She is long gone, replaced by the resilient thriver who gazes back at me from the mirror and lives a rich, fully, juicy life.

I ask myself, as do many of my single friends in their 50s and beyond, what if I am never in a full-out committed relationship?

I have just turned 61 and imagine I have another 20 some years left. What if I remain single for those decades? I am accepting that possibility as I might embrace an unpartnered life.

What would that look like, I ponder? Will I be one of those eccentric older women who lives an unconventional existence? I already do, according to my son. His "weird hippie mom" whose effusiveness, color, and pizazz, highlighted by purple hair, sometimes embarrasses him as much as it did when he was a teen. Will I be satisfied to have needs met in a patchwork style, with affection, attention, sex, and companionship arriving sporadically? Can I refrain from judging myself for being alone, since it seems no one else in my life casts disapproval on my single status?

I sometimes ask my intended, "Is this the day you will show up?" Am I hiding in plain sight despite feeling transparently, nakedly visible? People keep telling me that when I surrender attachment to outcome, this person will indeed knock on the door to my heart.

In the meantime, keeping my heart open to myself is essential. I am always and forever, the love of my life.

Originally published in The Huffington Post www.huffpost.com

What is your relationship status?

Are you content with your life as is?

How can you be your own best partner?

CHAPTER 13:

LADIES AND GENTLEMEN, START YOUR ENGINES

"Don't look for your dreams to become true; look to become true to your dreams." ~Michael Bernard Beckwith

I always get a shot of adrenaline hearing Wilber Shaw's classic line from 1953. (Note it was changed in 2016 to include Ladies)

So, you've done your due diligence on yourself. You've either made your mind up to attract a quality relationship or decided Singlehood is best for you. No right or wrong there, only you know what's best at this time for you.

The following is an exercise designed to help you attract "The One" or become the best YOU to date. Doing this daily changed my life. The greater your focus is on your goal, the greater your rewards. Roughly 40 years ago, I found a wonderful little book that changed my life forever, *The Strangest Secret* by the great Earl Nightingale. This was my first delve and taste into self-development. It's never failed me! I have listened to his audio CD more than 400 times, (available online and at most libraries) surprisingly, after all those times, I still hear new messages or things he mentioned that resonate even more deeply. In his classic book, Earl shares great lessons taught by some of the world's best teachers, including the story of Jesus' Sermon on the Mount. The key point here to remember is "Seek and Ye shall find. Knock and the door shall be opened unto you." I took that to mean regardless of my goal, if I knew what it was and worked towards it, it can happen. I speak from firsthand experience that this Magic happened for me. Many other great messengers also share this idea, Napoleon Hill in *Think and Grow Rich* and Rhonda Byrne in *The Secret* among them.

Mr. Nightingale then shared a fabulous analogy, he compared the human mind to the soil. While the mind is far more incredible than dirt, they work in the same way. He said the farmer plants corn and nightshade, (a deadly poison) in the ground. He takes care of his tiny seeds, waters and nurtures them. Voila, he grows corn and nightshade. Both came up. In the same way, the thoughts we keep in our mind are harbingers of things that can happen.

Now where am I going with this? I applied this technique in many areas of my life, from selling and winning sales contests, to purchasing my first home. I used it to help manifest my current marriage.

I visualized already being married, THIS IS KEY! The subconscious cannot differentiate what is real from VIVIDLY imagined. The secret is acting as if the thing in question already had happened. I am a coffee snob. I prefer dark, robust usually French roast coffees. Life is too short to drink crappy café.

Every morning for seven years since beginning this daily ritual, while making my daily morning Joe, I would go to the cabinet and faithfully pull out my future wife's coffee mug. This was a special coffee cup that I used for nothing else. I would set it on the counter awhile my Bunn coffee maker did its duty, and I already had the cream out. I would fill both cups. I would visualize, see CLEARLY in my mind's eye, bringing my beautiful wife her coffee. She smiled widely when I passed her the warm steaming mug. Here excited eyes slightly rolling back in her head as she tasted the day's first exquisite sip. She always thanked me with a kiss on the cheek. A man should know that the Bible dictates that it's his job to make the coffee for his mate. Don't believe me? Look up HEBREWS (that was supposed be funny).

Rituals create habits, once formed they are difficult to change. This technique can be applied to anything in life you want or aspire to be. Moreover, I didn't stop with the morning coffee visualization. I imagined other things happy couples did together, driving in the car, At dinner time I often would set the second plate out for my future wife. I kept the faith. I realize there are some skeptical people shaking their heads now. Understandably so, however the only way to find out if it works is to try it. What have you got to lose? Mine took seven years until we began dating however I knew she was "The One". I even gave her the coffee mug I used all those years and she LOVED hearing the story.

If you decide to try this, why not create your own lists of the things you want to attract into your life. Know the exact qualities your new partner will possess. If you want them to fill with happiness, see them laughing. If you envision yourself getting married one day, see yourself walking down the aisle, exchanging vows, hear them saying, "I do", kissing them, and then exchanging your rings. Watch yourself enjoying your honeymoon.

Let that glorious feeling surge throughout your entire being. The possibilities are endless!

If marriage isn't on your horizon, but you are still interested in a relationship, write down a detailed list of all the most desired qualities you are looking for in your mate. Again choose the most important ones and create your visualization using those, See it in vivid color. Watch it on the big screen like you're at the movies and that it has already happened. Perhaps you're at a romantic restaurant. Maybe preparing a meal together, watching a movie together, or sharing a nice bottle of champagne. Whatever you enjoy and desire is your ticket to ride. Be certain to be exact in your visualizations. Specificity yields greater rewards.

If you are content remaining single, no worries, this technique can easily work for your ideal situation as well. I would recommend writing down a list of all the things you are hoping for, rank them from most important to idle wishes, and start with the ones you have a burning desire to have. What changes are you looking to make within? Act as if they already have happened.

A great book that discusses Visualization is *The Magic of Thinking Big* by Claude M. Bristol. As the title suggests, go beyond your normal thinking. Stretch it. Don't be SHY, Be BOLD! There's real magic in doing so.

Think back to the chapter on "Emotional Gardening", this is nothing more than augmenting your emotional soil.

To this very day, I use various visualizations during my daily meditations. Some are healing for me or dear friends afflicted with health issues. Some are for greater prosperity; some are for helping the world by finding a cure and eliminating the COVID-19 virus.

My selfish wish is this book, like my others, help MILLIONS of people worldwide feel better about themselves and their current life. The key point here, is when I perform these, I already act as if they happened. I do them with the belief that I deserve these things and with my gifts I help others.

Moreover, while visualization techniques are incredibly helpful and attract one's burning desires, just hoping for any outcome is only partially helpful. One must do the physical work along with their visualizing. That's the real power.

For example, my burning desire for the last three years has been to get this book published. I had already done my research however the COVID-19 lockdown allowed me to begin in earnest the actual writing of chapters.

While I already saw it in the hands of its target audience and receiving RAVE reviews, I had to physically write it. I have a burning desire to do so. I think about it constantly during the day, different chapters, cover ideas, how to improve it, and so on. Still it requires me, Mr. ADHD, Mr.-can't- sit -still- for-long to put his ASS to chair daily. I set aside time daily to write. At night, usually between 2-4 AM I get up to use the restroom, make my little jaunt around the house to make sure everything is secure. Suddenly my mind is filled with ideas about the next chapter.

I don't let things stop me. For example, yesterday I was experiencing the nastiest pain in my right shoulder. I couldn't even sleep. It was strange as I hadn't done any heavy lifting in the day. I got maybe two hours of sleep the entire night. I was in incredible pain in the morning; luckily, my doctor was able to see me later in the day. It made it difficult to sit at my laptop, it was impossible to type with my dominant right hand, so I chicken pecked with my left hand. I forced myself to work on a chapter that I started. My caring wife drove me to the doctor's office where I was diagnosed, Turns out I have acute Subacromial Bursitis in my right shoulder, WTF? My doctor prescribed some Prednisone, a corticosteroid. It prevents the release of substances in the body that cause inflammation. I came home late and completed the chapter. No excuses. I used my pain for fuel, fired up with my burning desire to finish. Self-imposed deadlines are a marvelous kick in the butt for me.

This "take no prisoners" mindset works for me when something is important. I can gauge how important something is by counting the times during the day I am preoccupied with it. I keep a little note pad to capture ideas as they flow to me.

The question to ask yourself is how important is your goal? Are you willing to do the work required, to deal with the rejections that usually accompany dating and get back in the relationship ring?

Can you get knocked down eight times and get up nine? If you answered YES to all those telling questions, I have good news for you, your chances are excellent!

Before closing this chapter, I want to address something perhaps I should have earlier on concerning "FINDING THE ONE".

I realize there are probably people shaking their heads right now, thinking I'm full of it. I can appreciate why they might feel that way. Please allow me to dispel any misconception that I may have led you to believe. I use "Finding the One" as a colloquialistic premise; for me it means first finding yourself. This opens the doors to creating the dream. Once that happens, the flood gates of opportunity open wide.

Moreover with nearly eight billion people living today on Terra Firma, there are incredible possibilities; yours is out there.

Relationship expert Jennifer Blankl encourages exploration of this question: "How do you know you have found the one?"

"The seemingly romantic and fantasy concept of finding our one true and delicious love, in my humble and heartfelt opinion, sets us up for an extremely limited pool of options. The words and language we use are key in how we define things around us. It's how we define opportunities versus limitations. It's how we define what difficult and hard, versus what's easy and effortless. It helps us define what we deserve, versus what we foolishly and blindly believe we're unworthy of."

I concur with Jennifer's astute point, in my attempt to share what it takes to create the relationship of your dreams and finding the One.

I hope that you have picked up one of this book's major messages, which is you must first look deep inside yourself and take inventory. Delving deeply without judgment, resentment, or sadness as to what's happened to you. It already passed. You survived and it's time to move on taking the lessons with you.

In this way you reframe your pain, coming out from an injury to awakening and growth. Change your attitude about your past mistakes into the things you needed to experience.

The reason to do this healing exercise is that it is where the most important ONE dwells, and you always have. You see that person every time you look in the mirror. Once we establish a fully loving and accepting union between our intellectual and emotional side our larger over-self becomes one. Symmetry happens.

This inner congruency opens doors. This allows us to invite love in. Dr. Gary Salyer discusses this point in fabulous detail in his acclaimed book *Safe to Love Again: How to Release the Pain of Past Relationships and Create the Love You Deserve*. It offers a practical, step-by-step guide for creating the open-hearted space that allows love to emerge in your life. Dr. Gary will show you the path he has walked and acts as companion on your unique journey.

In closing, my wise friend Bre' Paletta puts it this way, "We do not manifest what we want; we manifest that which we are."

Do you believe that the one you are seeking is seeking you?

How will you recognize that person if they show up?

Can you be an energetic match for him or her?

CHAPTER 14:

THIRTY IMPORTANT QUESTIONS TO ASK BEFORE WE COMMIT BY EDIE WEINSTEIN

"The shortest distance between two people is a story."
~ Patti Digh

"To say that one waits a lifetime for his soulmate to come around is a paradox. People eventually get sick of waiting, take a chance on someone, and by the art of commitment become soulmates, which takes a lifetime to perfect." ~Criss Jami

This morning, I read an article that highlighted the reasons people find themselves, or perhaps lose themselves in relationships that are not a good fit. I noticed myself nodding in recognition as I ticked off the kinds of issues that clients I have seen as a therapist for the past three decades have presented in our sessions.

They range from not knowing the person in the mirror well enough, to being disillusioned by the person on the other side of the bed. While it would be easy to maintain my professional objectivity, what remains with me that is fodder for this post are how deeply and profoundly the concepts presented touch on my journey.

Married at 28, with a history of multiple relationships prior, widowed at 40, following a 12 year "paradoxical marriage," I have been ostensibly single for nearly 22 years, except for a few short-term relationships and friends with benefits interactions. I could chalk it up to the fear of loss and re-creating the worst dynamics of my marriage, analysis paralysis about what I did that contributed to some of the dysfunction in that decade-plus two, regret and shame about some of my choices, raising my son as a single parent, experimenting with relationship paradigm options, re-inventing myself, busy ness with life stuff, focusing on career building and at times, genuinely enjoying being single and now that my son is an adult, making choices that primarily affect only me.

I could second guess "If I knew then what I know now," and beat myself up over all the shoulda woulda coulda's and believe me, I have.

I would much rather explore and examine, from the perspective of being on the other side of the experience, not just what I want, but what I don't want, even though relationship experts generally encourage a focus on the positive. I am a believer, based on my own personal and professional perspective that I need to clear the detritus of previous encounters to build anew. So many people create new relationships on the wreckage of old interactions. As Joe Jackson sagely says, "You can't get what you want, 'til you know what you want."

There are questions I didn't ask myself in earlier years, both pre-and post-marriage and conversations that I wish I had back then. Of course, this seasoned woman has had time and life enough to make these queries. Perhaps they would be helpful for you as well.

What do I genuinely want in a relationship? Not what someone else thinks it should be. Not family, friends, or society. I'll live with myself 24/7 for the rest of my life and if I choose to blend my life with another's, that is crucial. My vivid imagination conjures up images of a dynamic, ever-growing "third entity" that combines the sum of the parts of the two of us.

At this point in my life, I have accumulated experiences and life lessons that I desire to share with a partner. I consider myself a wealthy woman since my friends and family are my treasures. The other person has "been there, done that, got the t-shirt" too. Together, we share the wealth.

How do I define a relationship?

My current definition involves two people who have a common and merged vision, who communicate it openly and who take steps daily to strengthen and support that bond. As a minister who has married over 300 couples since 1999, I have witnessed this dynamic with many of them. Although my parents came from "different sides of the track," with divergent socio-economic backgrounds, love and intention sustained their nearly 52-year marriage.

A huge dose of love, fun, affection in word and action, co-creating wonder, thinking of the other person and what will delight them, shared responsibility for maintaining a household, flexibility, willingness to work through "stuff" when things get messy, taking time and space to breathe and respond, rather than react and attack, knowing that we have each other's backs, open-mindedness, and openheartedness, creativity, play, spiritual practice, sexual nourishment, mutual support of each other's dreams (even if they are not in lockstep with each other's), are on my desire list.

What am I unwilling to accept?

Control, abuse, addiction, emotional manipulation, my own co-dependent tendencies taking hold, selling my soul for love, financial irresponsibility, lying, expectation that I act as caregiver and primary emotional strength in the relationship and that I clean up the "messes," literally or symbolically.

It's my take that relationship breakdown has a better chance of occurring because we don't ask certain questions from the get-go and instead, make assumptions that love is enough to sustain it. This isn't necessarily so. The questions to ask if you are face to face with a prospective partner and if asked of you, to be answered with naked honesty:

What models did you have for loving relationships when you were growing up?

What did you learn from them and what did you learn from those that weren't healthy?

What did you learn about self-love?

How was love expressed in your childhood?

If you were a survivor of abuse, how have you done your healing work?

If addiction was present in your family, how has it impacted on you?

How do you want your relationship to mirror that of your parents and how do you want it to differ?

If someone disagrees with you, how do you face it?

When things don't go the way you want, how do you handle disappointment?

How do you express emotion, most especially anger?

What was the best thing that ever happened in your life?

What was the worst thing that ever happened in your life?

How do you deal with change?

What brings you joy and satisfaction?

What are your values — particularly social?

How do you take care of yourself physically, emotionally, mentally, and spiritually?

If you want to have children, what is your take on child-rearing when it comes to discipline and consequences?

How do you face a loss?

When the inevitable dark nights of the soul occur, what sustains you until the morning comes?

What are your spiritual beliefs? (For some who see themselves as atheist or agnostic, what enlightens and enlivens you and from where do you get your sustenance?)

Let's talk about our sexual desires, experiences, and needs.

I am a big believer in full disclosure, knowing that there is a difference between secrecy and privacy. Without needing to disclose the names of all previous lovers and interactions, it is important that a partner know if there are others still in your life. Safer sex practices are crucial as well.

If you were in a committed relationship that shifted, how has your heart healed and are you ready for a new one?

Do you remain friends with former partners? (By the way, I see that as a strength if the friendships are healthy and not fraught with jealousy and manipulation.)

How do you balance needs for "we time" and "me time," so that you nourish yourself as well as the relationship?

How do you use your resources…saver, spender, sharer with money, time, and energy?

Do you want a relationship, or do you need a relationship?

Who are you without one?

Of course, these are inquiries that take place over time and not all at once on a first date. The professional interviewer in me laughs at the Ally Mc Beal internal dialog absurdity of that scenario.

This was initially published in Elephant Journal. www.elephantjournal.com

Have you ever had this kind of conversation with potential partners?

Are you willing?

Can you add other questions to the list?

CHAPTER 15:

HURRAY! YOU BELIEVE YOU HAVE FOUND THE ONE, NOW WHAT?

"If you would be loved, love,
and be loveable."
~ Benjamin Franklin

Finally, your time has come. You can't believe it, you've already pinched yourself 111 times, and you're awake. It finally happened. You are a couple.

You truly feel that this person is THE ONE.

Let's assume for a moment you have done all your mental and emotional due diligence and you have set the groundwork that will allow you to create and enjoy the best relationship you have ever been in.

You have done the required inner work. You took the appropriate time to grieve (if your last one ended badly so this is not merely one on the rebound.) You have forgiven yourself for your shortcomings that may have escalated your last break up.

You have worked on yourself sufficiently which has helped create a loving relationship within yourself.

You have fully accepted yourself and can say you are the most important person in your life. You love yourself more than you have ever allowed yourself to in your past.

You have physically met this person; it wasn't just an online, long-distance relationship. You are both sure you haven't fallen prey to the 'in love with love' trap. You have spent face to face time getting to know them. You both believe that you have seen the genuine person and not just the persona.

You both know yourselves completely; exactly who you are, your core needs that you both are looking to have fulfilled in Mental, Physical, Emotional, Spiritual, Social, Physical, Financial, Family, and Career realms.

While there is never a guarantee that all of the items on your relationship wish list will be checked off, ideally many of these will be.

You both share similar moral values and compasses.

You both can easily admit when you're wrong; admitting fault, and neither of you have any problems apologizing to each other.

You both know about each other's core values and you're certain that your potential long-term relationship matches each other on all levels.

You both share similar views on life and lifestyles, politics, diet, personalities, religious and/or spiritual commonalties, cleanliness habits, smoking preferences, and alcohol/drug preferences, and so on.

You both have been honest in sharing medical issues and/or history.

You both have learned how to effectively communicate with each other.

You both truly take time to listen to the other.

You both enjoy spending time with each other, doing nothing, in particular, per se.

You both have accepted each other's flaws, shortcomings, personality disorders, quirks, weirdness, idiosyncrasies, differences, and you still love each other.

You both share a deep-rooted mutual respect.

You both share similar ideas about monogamy or not as well as marriage.

You both see the other as their equal partners.

You both feel comfortable in social settings together. Note: Be aware if either of you have any social anxieties.

If either of you has children, you both have accepted each other's as your own, as well as having discussed whether you both want children, now, sometime in the future or never. Would they be your procreation, or would you consider adoption?

You've already had a disagreement or misunderstanding and know how to work through it.

You both have set boundaries and are willing to abide by them.

You both know each other's Love Languages.

You both feel you're compatible enough to live with each other.

You have met one another's family and friends (where possible) and they are accepting of you both.

You both have shared any pressing concerns you each have about any subjects which you each deem important and vital to discuss openly.

You both have shared your financial concerns.

You both are comfortable giving each other the space you each require, not needing to be together every living second of the day.

You both have the same idea of what commitment entails as you have read Edie's chapter on the thirty things to discuss before committing.

You both can envision spending the rest of your lives with the other.

If you can honestly say you have addressed every one of these points and others not even broached here and you both agree you are ready...then I say, Pop that Champagne. Mazel Tov and Congratulations.

What feelings arise when you think about having intense conversations?

For some, it is like diving into the deep end of the pool. Can you trust that you will be each other's lifeguards?

How do you imagine it will be once you swim to the other side together?

CHAPTER 16:

THE DIFFERENCE BETWEEN BEING ALONE AND LONELY

"Loneliness expresses the pain of being alone,
and solitude expresses the glory of being alone."
~Paul Tillich

Holidays can bring us our highest highs as well as our lowest lows. I am sharing the following story as I feel the suggestions which I gave to my buddy are applicable and can benefit any relationship.

It was New Year's Eve a few years ago, when I received a heartfelt text from an old friend that I hadn't seen in years. It makes me incredibly happy that distance hasn't diminished our longtime friendship. Even if we hadn't spoken in years; when we start talking it's like we just chatted yesterday. He wished me a Happy New Year and asked me to give him a call when I had a chance.

This wasn't like him and I called him immediately.

He thanked me for calling so quickly, and we exchanged pleasantries. My buddy was acting cordial, but there was an unusual undertone in his voice. He wasn't his normal upbeat self, and he wasn't drinking that I could tell.

I asked him what was going on. The conversation suddenly got serious. He mentioned that around the holidays he gets depressed; that he felt that something was missing from his life, that he was lacking something. I listened quietly. He mentioned that he practices much self-diagnosis; he reads many uplifting Facebook postings which help temporarily, but they don't fulfill him. He confided he loves his wife dearly and feels blessed for his children; he doesn't take them or his future for granted. He paid me a huge compliment saying he envied me and believed that I have found inner peace. He desperately wants to find it too. While his comments are appreciated, I must confess, in my past I had often struggled with my inner self created demons. Mostly mine deal with grieving, hurt feelings from poor communication leading to misunderstandings, lack of a meaningful romantic relationship and my preoccupation with my professional career. I had a total A 'hole supervisor who took pleasure in making my life miserable. Rumor has it, the man died several years ago with very few friends.

Having struggled with nagging, tempestuous bouts of depression, fueled by seething anger issues, I completely understand how personal challenges can bring one down into the depths of despondency. One can feel hopeless over them. The good news is that there are many tools and techniques to help alleviate one's suffering. While there is no known magical formula or one fix-all solution that can make everyone's immediate problems disappear, they can be lessened in duration and intensity.

My buddy knew that years ago I was on the brink of cashing in my chips, as didn't see a reason to live. I was embarrassed to admit that fact. It was a very dark and dour period in my life.

He is also aware that I'm not a licensed therapist. Nor did I ever claim any ideas I suggested were right, only that they have been saving graces for me.

Before I share my ideas that I had with him that day, I would advise and respectfully request that if you the reader are dealing with deep depression issues, things that thwart your daily happiness, PLEASE seek some professional help. It doesn't make one weak by admitting they are dealing with heavy issues. It means they are strong enough to receive help. Open-minded people will admit that they are finally ready to deal with these agonizing, debilitating problems.

Rest assured that your friends and hopefully your family will support your wise decision.

I mentioned the following to my buddy that I have six things I will share in no specific order. He asked me to continue. I told him that the single greatest tool I've found immediate relief and benefit from is "Daily Meditation" (sometimes called prayer or deep introspection) While there are hundreds of different kinds of ways to do it, only you will know which method will work best for you.

Next I told him another great technique that anyone can do anytime or anyplace is to simply focus on the breath.

Sounds simple, I know, however it truly works and has been disseminated for thousands of years by the wisest teachers.

It matters not whether one is religious or not, race, creed, or sex play no part in the relief daily meditation practice can provide.

Next mentioned was gratitude, the miracle cure. I begin my day by reviewing in my mind the 20 things which I am grateful for. I also do this anytime I'm feeling down. Many times I give thanks repetitively, for the love in my life, my friends, my health, having a roof over my head, my daughters, being employed, etc. At this point in our evolution, we can only focus fully on one thought completely at a time. Focusing on what one is grateful for helps one regain and connect with inner peace. The transformative healing power of gratitude is life changing. Being profoundly grateful for all my blessings has helped me deal with the devastating lingering feelings from the myriad deaths I've recently experienced.

Then I mentioned life purpose; when I hit the big 5-0, I discovered something that changed my daily life. I finally figured out what my life purpose was. It has made me feel whole. It's given me a reason to give more of myself. Only you can answer this burning question, why are you here? What will you be your legacy, what will you be remembered for? If you can clearly define your life purpose in 10 words or less, congratulations: you're in the top 5% in the entire world. I commend you! My life purpose is helping others to define theirs. I work towards my purpose each day. Don't worry if you're not sure exactly what yours is or that yours may have changed. It gives you something to ponder and discover. This one insight is perhaps the greatest gift you could ever give yourself. It gives meaning to one's daily existence.

Next was random acts of kindness; especially to people (or animals), that can never repay you. When

I'm feeling low, I reach out and touch people. It's not hard to give a kind word, a smile. How one treats people they don't have to be nice to defines them to a T.

Lastly is forgiveness; when we carry the burden of non-forgiveness, we are the ones that suffer. Forgiveness doesn't mean forgetting the past. We forgive others not because they deserve it, rather because we deserve peace. By doing so, we release a heavy burden. It takes a stronger person to do so. It's not easy. This doesn't mean we have to be around folks who caused us pain.

I acknowledge what happened and try to remember their good points, after all I did enjoy a better relationship with them at one time. I don't hate them; I simply choose not to have them in my life.

These are but a few ideas that have helped me battle my ego and manic behaviors. Sharing my daily blog, writings, etc. is my ongoing spiritual therapy.

One never knows how sharing what's affecting them can help others they don't even know are suffering.

My buddy was silent and seemed to be considering what I shared; it was a lot to take in at once. He thanked me and said he'd give them a try.

I talked to him right before I finished writing this chapter. I let him know his story was being added to my book, with his consent. My phone went silent; he asked if his name was not being mentioned, right? I assured him it wasn't. A sigh of relief could be felt through thousands of miles of cell phone technology. He said he appreciated the ideas we shared that day. He was happy to report that he finally got some counseling which helped him immediately, he felt like his therapist helped him to be able to concisely share the things that were bothering him and gave him exercises to deal with his angst. Having done so, he felt he had a closer relationship with his wife. He finally shared things with her he never had the courage to do before and she was totally accepting of it and she wishes he had done so years ago.

He started doing the things he used to do for his wife before they got married. He said in some ways, he feels like they are dating again. He went on to say, this last Christmas was one of the best one in years that he could remember. He has added several projects and hobbies that he'd always wanted to do which gives him joy and a sense of accomplishment. Before we hung up I complimented him having the courage to address his issues and that he had worked on them. He mentioned that it was the best thing he had ever done for himself and looked forward to reading my book.

Thomas E. Ziemann

What rituals and practices do you engage in?

How do you feel afterward?

What happens if you skip a day or two?

CHAPTER 17:

CLEAR AND PRESENT...BOUNDARIES

*"Daring to set boundaries is about having
the courage to love ourselves,
even when we risk disappointing others."*
~Brene Brown

One of the biggest lessons I had to learn and relearn the hard way was to respect other people's boundaries and creating my own.

If you know me, I am a touchy-feely guy. Some people like or at least accept it. Some have asked me not to touch them or give them more room as I have invaded their space. This used to bother me as I meant no harm by touching. I didn't respect their personal space and that was my bad. Back in my formative years I was the kid everyone liked to pick on, belittle, and tease incessantly. I had no real friends to speak of. To become more popular, I became a people pleaser. I had a hard time saying NO even when it was to my detriment. Others would mention, "Hey man, you're too nice. You let people walk all over you. They don't respect you. They think it makes you appear weak. They mock you behind your back." Now that devastated me. Sadly those obsequious, overly fawning habits and behavior followed me into my 20s. What was even worse, I was seen as a pariah by several women I had an interest in. I spent too much money trying to impress them and buy their love and affection. It never lasted, leaving me even more broke and feeling like an abject failure concerning my relationships. Something happened that changed my life. I read Dale Carnegie's classic book, *How To Win Friends and Influence People.* While I was friendly, I lacked the skills to be liked. Once I took on his powerful ideas, things improved drastically. It taught me was that I didn't have to be someone's doormat to have their approval. It also taught me to set my boundaries. No longer was it important if people liked me, what mattered more was that I did. There is a fine line between healthy ego and narcissistic behaviors. Not being invested in others' immediate approval stopped much of what felt like rejection. Magically when I started caring for myself so did others. It empowered me. And I didn't have to act like an ass when someone asked me to do something I didn't want to. I took my power back and wasn't seen as an easy target anymore. I had an epiphany; healthy relationships have boundaries.

Setting boundaries changed my life. It meant that I had learned to communicate more effectively coming from a place of power, not swayed by others' attempts to manipulate me anymore. Great advice I once heard was establishing healthy boundaries in any relationship allows both partners to feel equally comfortable. Besides, it helps develop positive self-esteem; thereby creating a lasting, more meaningful bond. Trust is also established when both partners respect each other's boundaries. One way to do this is by learning to effectively communicate, telling them exactly how you feel or what you mean. Be aware of some people's mind game that if you do what I just mentioned then they will decry that you don't love them. If that is their response, a simple question to ask is this, "If you felt I loved you, what would I be saying or doing differently?"

We all make mistakes, owning up to them creates trust. Walk your talk, live up to your word. As Maslow taught, doing so demonstrates congruence where deeper trust occurs.

Abraham Maslow was an acclaimed American psychologist who was best known for creating Maslow's Hierarchy of Needs, a theory of psychological health predicated on fulfilling innate human needs in priority, culminating in self-actualization. What made him special was that his thinking was original. Most psychologists before him had been concerned with pathology. Maslow described human needs as ordered in a proponent hierarchy—a pressing need would have to be mostly satisfied before someone would give their attention to the next highest need.

One especially important thing to remember is no one is a mind reader nor can we guess our partner's feelings. Sure we can generalize, and because we know them we falsely believe we know best or what they meant.

Real communication skills avoid the guesswork trap and create deeper intimacy. Masterful communicators never assume they know for sure what the other means. They use reflective listening, repeating what they believe they heard. This proactive communication is magical, try it for yourself.

My friend Marc always has ample wisdom to share. He never forces it. When he sees I'm disturbed, he asks questions, listens intently then gives a few choice tidbits. On one occasion, we were sitting back in my back yard. It was a beautiful Pacific Northwest late spring day. The primroses were seducing our olfactory senses with a dreamy perfume that wafted throughout the yard.

We were tipping back a few icy cold St. Pauli Girls and solving the problems of the world. He knew something was eating at me and said, "Tom, what's bothering you?" I assured him it wasn't him, nor was it a big deal although this was an ongoing issue that I wanted to get his thoughts on.

We have a mutual friend. On the positive side, the guy's very charismatic, charming, and funny, a great storyteller, however, it's generally all about him. Where he just traveled. What big account he landed for his company, what concert he had tickets for. Rarely did he ever ask us how we were doing.

We would share a story and per usual, he didn't appear to be listening, rather he would check his cell phone and send multiple texts during the conversation. Nodding every so often as if he were truly listening. Often he would interrupt us to tell his "better story". It got really old.

This guy is a classic narcissist. I know because I was one too. He is extremely sensitive if you call him on it. The great stand-up comedian Brian Regan has an uproarious funny skit called "The Me Monster" which describes our friend to a T. If you caught a tasty spring Chinook on the Willamette, he caught a larger one on the Columbia. I started sharing his latest diatribe and Marc stopped me. He already knew who I was talking about even though I hadn't mentioned his name. He asked if it bothered me this much then why the hell did I hang around with him? I started making excuses for him. He stopped me again and said, "I know how ya feel. That used to bother me as well. I have a solution." At this time, my Dobermans were up, and I listened with surgical focus on every word. He mentioned that we all have choices of who we spend time with. If we go into our relationship knowing who the person is, what behaviors they have previously demonstrated, then we aren't surprised anymore. It doesn't affect us in the same way anymore.

BINGO... that was powerful. I remember his sage advice as though it was yesterday. Of course, he was correct.

Author Mark Manson reminds us that, "Healthy personal boundaries= taking responsibility for your actions and emotions, while not taking responsibility for the actions or emotions of others."

In *The Department of Zenitation*, in Chapter 127, I said, "Boundaries, we all have them. Be they physical, emotional, spiritual, philosophical, or mental, they exist within us. Why do we have them?"

Some reasons are fairly obvious. We have been hurt and won't allow anyone the privilege of doing that again. We can't always be nice, by doing so, we allow unscrupulous people to take advantage of us, so we must set boundaries. Ego plays a big part on occasion. Sometimes it's with a person we've just met, we won't allow them to know the real us until they've gained our trust. Or it might be that we don't like or trust the other party and have no interest in opening up. "It's none of their business to know anything about me," is the thought. There is no right or wrong answer, the spirit will move us in many directions for many reasons. Sometimes, it's prudent to be on guard and cautious of another person's intentions.

Here are a few ideas. First, be careful of the questions you ask people that you have just met.

Second, people's opinion of you doesn't matter; to thine own self be true.

Third, my boundaries are different than others. It's better not to violate theirs and create an enemy. Knowing your motivations for doing anything cleanses your soul.

In closing, think about these boundaries to consider when entering a new relationship. Share your mutual expectations; let them know what you expect out of your relationship and what you will do in return. Then live up to your word. Discuss personal tolerances. We are all different in this department. When you're comfortable and getting to the point of taking your relationship to the physical, share your ideas about sex. Other things to bring up are your family, friends, ideas about a potential future together, what you want and then listen to theirs. It's critical to make it crystal clear what your deal breakers are.

Being willing to have these kinds of frank discussions does many things aside from establishing clear boundaries. It sets the bar early on, that way there is no mystery and helps to avoid misunderstandings, conflicts, and expectations later on.

What do boundaries mean to you?

Do you allow people to cross yours?

Do you stand your ground?

CHAPTER 18:

BREAKUPS AND DIVORCE

"Divorce isn't such a tragedy. A tragedy's staying in an unhappy marriage, teaching your children the wrong things about love. Nobody ever died of divorce."
~ Jennifer Weiner

The sad fact is that according to the National Survey of Family Growth PolitiFact.com estimated in 2012 that the lifelong probability of a marriage ending in divorce is 40%–50%. That's a staggering figure. It sky rocked during the 1960s to the 80s. In 2018, there were more than 782,038 divorces. Studies I've read online stated the average age was only 30 years old and that the divorce rate amount couples over age 50 have doubled since the '90s. Divorces tended to peak during the spring and summer.

The Census Bureau stated that in 2018, there were more than 13.4 million parents separated from the child's other parent. Even more depressing was among parents who have child support agreements, less than half received the full amount of support they're entitled to.

What's up with that???

It surprised me to hear that *The Atlantic* and *Psychnet* reported that children whose parents fought a lot but stayed together are more likely to divorce than children whose parents divorced.

I've always contended that it's much easier to get divorced than to get married. Many hold the belief that divorce is preferable to staying in an unhappy marriage. In an article entitled "11 Reasons Why Divorce Is Better Than Staying In A Bad Marriage," author and Senior Lifestyle Editor at Huffington Post, Brittany Wong shares the wisdom of other HuffPost bloggers on the subject. They range from divorce opening doors to meeting someone new, to divorce offering a new lease on life, from being a happier parent to setting a good example for your children.

I used to believe that sexual infidelity was the leading cause of relationships and marriages failing. Research has shown me that communication problems was the number one reason. Other causes include alcohol or drug abuse, gambling addiction, and social media.

Workaholism, defined as working 70-80 hours per week has been reported as a detriment to some marriages as one spouse put above their work priorities over that of their relationship.

In surveys I've read, money was cited as the one thing couples argue about. Issues such as financial infidelity, credit card debt, overextending financial resources, impulse buying binges, and unexpected expenses all played a role as well.

Top 12 reasons people stated they got divorced:

Poor communication

Abuse- mental, physical, emotional

Money issues

Irreconcilable differences

Infidelity

Lack of compatibility

Lack of intimacy

Constant fighting

Addictions

Weight gain

Unwilling to work on the relationship

Mental illness

Some people stay together because of their children. I've read that divorce may be better for their children; growing up in a happy home is more likely to protect them from mental, physical, educational, and social problems. When they witness constant arguing, or perhaps one parent pitting the kids against the other using them as emotional pawns, it contributes to sadness that can deeply affect them, creating long-standing emotional issues.

One positive note is that in 2020, divorce rates were dropping slightly.

Several sources noted these statistics Divorce Statistics in the US.

The idea that 50% of all marriages end in divorce was prevalent in the 1980s but research shows a decline in the rate of divorce since then. Not including those who get legally separated, this is the statistical breakdown

First Marriages: 42-45 % will terminate with a divorce as the result.

Second Marriages: 60 % will terminate with a divorce as the result.

Third Marriages: 73 % will terminate with a divorce as the result.

I bring up those grim points not to depress you, far from it. Awareness of the contributing factors for divorce may help prevent it and understanding why they happen can help remedy the problems before they get worse.

They can help one make better choices before getting married such as not getting married too young and choosing a long-term compatible mate who shares similar values and in-common lifestyle choices. Religious beliefs, political leanings, sexual compatibility, whether you both want children all are serious matters to consider before that walk down the aisle. My advice is to marry your best friend. Friendship is at the core of any lasting romantic relationship.

I would also recommend that couples get marital and financial counseling beforehand; it will make you wiser and give your marriage a better chance to last and thrive.

Recognizing the warning signs is a blessing if you are serious about relationship repair. This has to be a combined effort; both spouses have to be on board.

It's not going be all fun and games, we all experience ebbs and flow concerning our relationships. You are going to know each other's flaws and faults. Focus on what you love about the other and what brought you together initially.

If something bothering you, figure out a way to share it immediately and calmly. If your communication skills are lacking, work on yourself. There are many great books out there that can help.

The 5 Love Languages by Dr. Gary Chapman

How to Live With Another Person by Dr. David Viscott

Getting the Love You Want: A Guide for Couples by Harville Hendrix, Ph.D.

The Seven Principles for Making Marriage Work by Dr. John M. Gottman

Hold Me Tight: Seven Conversations for a Lifetime of Love by Sue Johnson, EdD .

Talk to Me Like I'm Someone You Love: Relationship Repair in a Flash by **Nancy Dreyfus**, Psy.D.

Safe To Love Again by Gary Salyer, Ph.D.

If you still can't come to a resolution and it's to the point where you or your spouse are ready to hang up their spurs then get help IMMEDIATELY. Not just friendly advice from well-meaning friends. Find professional guidance. You both have too much invested.

I've heard numerous stories where one partner is interested in getting help and the other reluctantly goes to therapy to avoid being perceived as not wanting to work on the marriage, while deep inside they have already mentally and romantically checked out and are eying the exit door.

Recently, I was talking to a friend about his two divorces. His story was interesting in that he was very upbeat about his ex-wife; in fact according to him, they are better friends now than in their previous two attempts. Yes, he married the same woman twice. I asked him to explain what happened. He said he married his grammar school sweetheart shortly after high school. They had been together for 10 years. Sadly within a year, their marriage was on the rocks and they divorced shortly after that. He cited being too much of a party animal, not understanding what responsibilities came with his wedding vows, and looking back, was far too young.

He joined the military, grew up, and after he was honorably discharged he struck up another relationship with his ex-wife. This time both were supposedly more emotionally and mentally mature. He, due to serving his country, and she had gone off to college and got her degree. They had five great years, had kids but started drifting apart again. He mentioned he was putting more time into growing his burgeoning company than focused on her needs. In his mind at the time he thought he was making a sacrifice for his young family, sometimes working 90 hours a week, never taking time for the family he said he loved. Three years later they divorced a second time. He stated irreconcilable differences as their reason. I pushed for more details; he simply said they had grown apart.

On a brighter note, he has stayed close friends with his former wife. They still share parental custodial duties, plus he's incredibly financially responsible concerning paying child support. They live less than a block away from each other. Both have since remarried and he told me they get along well with each other's new spouses.

I also asked if he ever felt uncomfortable being around his ex's husband. He smiled and said, "Tom, he's a good man. He treats my children as his own. Plus he treats her with respect and tenderness. He loves her deeply, it's obvious. It's what real friends want for each other." I was touched hearing that.

One other short story my friend shared was during his second divorce he got some sage advice from an old friend of his, a man who had been married 25 years. He inquired how he did it. How did he stay happily married for a quarter of a century? His buddy said he married five times. Now, my friend knew that to be untrue but let him finish. His friend said it seemed to him that his relationship had changed about every five years; his wife was seemly a different person. He rolled with the changes. He worked on their differences. Picked and chose his battles wisely. He instinctively knew when something was worth arguing about and when to shut his mouth. He summed it all up in two words, "effective communication" between them.

I found his stories compelling on many fronts. Perhaps his is a rare situation. It gave me hope for others who have divorced, that they too might be able to take a page out of my friend's playbook for their happiness.

Forgiveness of yourself and your ex will help you come to terms with some closure. We do this not because they deserve it, we do if for ourselves to give us inner peace.

Another good point I took away from his story is that we all change. We are not the same people who said, "I do."

Our needs may be different at 40 than they were our 20s.

My buddy Marc mentioned something I never forgot. He said, "Tom, none of us stay young and pretty forever," I pondered that thought for many months. He was right of course, however, the deeper meaning I gleaned seems like a perfect way to end this chapter.

My advice is to marry for more than looks, status, and money. If you want real happiness and for your marriage to last, choose smartly. Remember they take daily work to keep them fresh and alive. By doing so, you can achieve that Dream Relationship you have been desiring evermore.

If you are divorced, what were the reasons for it?

What have you learned from the person you once promised to love forever?

Can you learn to forgive what you can't go back and change that will enable you to move forward?

CHAPTER 19:

COVID-19, THE FURY, AND ITS BEAUTY

"For every action, there is an equal and opposite reaction."
~Sir Isaac Newton

Back in early January of 2020 was the first time I can recall hearing about the dreaded Coronavirus.

My morning alarm clock had gone off. NPR was reporting something causing major panic which caught my immediate attention. Reports were coming out of Wuhan, China that a deadly, infectious disease called COVID-19 was spreading quickly. It was caused by severe acute respiratory syndrome coronavirus 2 (SARS-CoV-2).

At that point, I wasn't sure as to the severity of this. I would be certain to listen for future stories hoping it was a flash in the pan and disappear much like the Swine Flu had decades before.

Sadly, it did not go away; instead, it began to spread like wildfire and went global. This resulted is the first worldwide pandemic that I would be affected by and hopefully the last.

Many of the Far-Right News outlets were calling this a hoax, no more dangerous than the common Flu and that we had little to be concerned about.

My gut told me otherwise. I was skeptical about their false assumptions and attempts to brush this under the rug. I started hearing daily from different sources just how many deaths were being attributed to this COVID-19 virus.

Fast forward…

In May 2020, more than 3.93 million cases have been reported across 187 countries and territories, resulting in more than 274,000 deaths.

Entire countries had taken this SERIOUSLY. National lockdowns had been created to slow the spread of the virus. Millions of people worldwide were out of work.

In April, NPR reported that the U.S Unemployment Rate had risen to a Record 14.7%! This staggering event created an unprecedented 20.5 million jobs were shed as the coronavirus pandemic hit our economy. Many experts were suggesting it was much higher than it had been reported. The U.S. hadn't seen this many unemployment claims since the Great Depression of the 1930s. Non-essential companies were ordered closed. People were out of work and told to remain in their homes. Hoarding of food and household items had created nationwide panic. Store shelves had been decimated. No toilet paper, Lysol disinfectant, Kleenex, paper towels, bread flour, or even yeast was to be found.

Physical distancing had become the norm and people were wearing facial masks as been seen in other parts of the world.

Doom and Gloom was the call of the day.

Michelle and I were some of the lucky people that had managed to keep our jobs. The respective companies we work for had the optimism and bright vison to see that this would one day end. So both large corporations asked the lion's share of their employees to work from home. The ones considered essential continued working as before only taking newly imposed precautions.

Throughout this entire escapade, I kept a positive attitude. I counted my blessings daily. Much like Einstein did during his daily walk around Princeton University, I too tried to come up with 100 reasons to give thanks. Michelle and I would play the Gratitude game, simply stated we would take turns naming something we were grateful for. The only rule was you couldn't use the same blessing your partner had just used. The winner was the one who spoke last and got a 20-minute massage. I had never received so many back rubs since before getting married.

I continued to focus on the positive things that were being reported, such as that the ozone hole above the Antarctic had shrunk significantly. Scientists said it is on the road to recovery.

Animal shelters reported a major boost in foster applications which we two animal lovers applauded since we met as a result of a fundraiser for an animal rescue program. Work has begun on a graphene-based sieve that will produce drinking water from seawater.

Scientists report that sustainable nuclear fusion is just around the corner. We're remarkably close to having medication that can cure Autism symptoms. Businesses found brand new ways to innovate and increased revenue.

My wife Michelle has been delighted that Hallmark which is her number one network created "Christmas in March" showing all her favorite movies. Moreover It had never been easier to stream and watch movies and actual theater in the privacy of one's home. I got to watch my GUY FLICKS as Michelle calls them, like the last *Terminator* film, my favorite Sci-Fi programs; *West World, Picard, Star Trek Discovery*, and the new version of *Lost In Space*.

Young people were delivering food and other items to vulnerable populations. People sent out uplifting cards and handwritten letters of hope to residents in nursing homes. Disneyland donated its excess food to food banks. TV medical dramas donated movie set supplies to real hospitals and clinics. A cat film festival raised money for Indie movie theaters.

Oprah Winfrey, President Barack Obama, and Steven Spielberg addressed 2020 graduates with virtual shout outs. A man raced 20.20 miles to raise money for graduates who couldn't afford to buy their yearbooks.

A few wildlife sightings were enthusiastically shared across social media, sunny news indeed amid the bleak reality of the Coronavirus pandemic. Wild dolphins and swans had returned to the canals in Italy, something that hadn't been witnessed in many years.

Los Angeles, California had reported unprecedented smog-free skies. The 101 and I-5 have never been this easy to drive on in 50 years.

People were staying at home with loved ones. They were reading together as a family. They were making and enjoying meals under one roof. They spent time talking to one another as opposed to zombified television viewing and gaming. They were playing board games and making the most of their confinement quarantine status.

In an era of the increasing prevalence of burnout, people were reported getting better sleep, eating better, and learning to relax a wee bit more, taking one day at a time.

My longtime Facebook friend Terrance Ellis wrote this:

"We are experiencing a major shift in the way we treat one another and nature. Open hearts are awakening closed ones of others as kindness penetrates. This is an opportunity for so many to raise their level of consciousness to higher levels through the power of love."

Ironically, that COVID-19 period had become a blessing for me.

It gave me the kick in the ass I needed to begin tackling things I had been procrastinating for years, such as finishing this book. It allowed me the time to fix things around the house that I was ignoring. It gave me more time to spend enjoying our outdoor sanctuary, feed the Koi several times daily, and work to beautify its ten separate garden areas. Our ten cats never had more time with us daily; they were all in great spirits and health.

It also allowed Michelle and I to become even closer. We used our time together creatively and constructively; we worked to keep our relationship stronger. We cooked meals together, played music for each other, made TikToc videos, did weekly ZOOM video chats with Michelle's family and put phone calls on speakerphone so that we both could be a part of each other's conversations with out of state friends, thereby creating a deeper emotional and loving bond between us.

One measure of the nature of your relationship is if your partner is someone with whom you would enjoy being quarantined. **I must admit how lucky I am to have Michelle to have gone through it with.**

The point here is regardless of any circumstance, there are always positive things that come as a direct result. Relationships end, new ones blossom. Jobs end, new employment is generally found with better opportunities.

It's up to us to look for life's blessings and lessons.

No doubt the COVID-19 period was difficult for people who were separated by a long-distance relationship. Indeed

Internet dating was tough as well. I have always been of the opinion it was far better to meet potential relationship people as soon as you both felt comfortable doing so. Zoom Dating became an accepted way for each person to get to know the other better.

NPR broadcast an insightful half hour program called; "Love On Lockdown: Tips For Dating During The Coronavirus Crisis," which can be Googled to hear or read it. The New York Times published an interesting article as well called "How Coronavirus Is Changing the Dating Game for the Better". Both of these sources put a positive spin on dating during the COVID-19 pandemic.

How would you describe life in the time of COVID-19?

Have your relationships changed as a result?

How have you adapted to your 'now normal'?

CHAPTER 20:

HOLD MY BEER, DON JUAN

"The biggest coward of a man
is to awaken the love of a woman
without the intention of loving her."
~Bob Marley

Picture this…you and your love are on the vacation destination of a lifetime. Something you've only dreamed of and you're both here!

It's midafternoon on a beautiful European summer day. You just walked into one of Paris's renowned restaurants; "Le Bistro Parisian" known for its incredible food, ambiance, and service. A place you saw on the Travel Channel and have been dying to try. This hopping hot spot has been booked solid for weeks, tourists relish this gem for its friendliness, superior service, tasty gourmet meals, beautifully presented plates, gorgeous décor plus its reasonable prices.

You however lucked out; five minutes before you called, they had a last-minute cancellation which you jumped on post-haste. The Maître d, who speaks impeccable English with a deep sensual French accent, welcomes you to Paris's finest restaurant. He asks if you have a reservation. You tell him your name. He checks his reservation book, "ah, we just spoke." He smiles and beckons you to follow him, in one hand he's holding two freshly printed, ornate menus dated that day the other, a large, well-worn dark brown, leather-bound wine list. He shows you to his best outdoor table and welcomes you to please sit down, holding the chair for your date. You both are now sitting out on the freshly painted deck; unique artwork and plants abound. A welcoming table adorning a brand-new white table linen, shiny silverware peaks though tightly wrapped cloth napkins await you both. The Maître d nods at one of his well-dressed attentive staff members who quickly and cheerfully bring you tall glasses of lemon Perrier, small sprigs of spearmint dance above the bubbly effervesce.

You knew you didn't order them. Without hesitation the wait staffs young man mentions;

"Compliments of the house. Bien Accueillir. Welcome to Le Bistro Parisian."

Suddenly, another wait staff member approaches the table and she smiles widely as she puts down an attractive breadbasket handmade of willow.

A small brass label on the front denoted "Matfer Bourgeat" a French designer basket containing different types of freshly baked bread, still warm from the oven from "Boulangerie Utopie", one of Frances best-known bakeries, world-renowned for their baguettes and crusty dinner rolls. The heavenly smells of those oblong mini loaves waft all around you. Your quivering taste buds were watering at that time.

While breaking into the pieces of bread, smearing unsalted butter wildly on them, you notice that you are sitting directly above the famous Sienne River. You can see numerous brightly colored tiny pleasure crafts, scant sailboats, and large cargo ships motoring up and down its calm, green alluring waters. An occasional gull caws in the distance. The Eiffel Tower is within walking distance which glimmered and majestically shimmered brightly from the late afternoon sun. You're pinching yourselves; you made it, you're really here, sitting in Paris, enjoying a magical moment. Your waiter saunters over and introduces himself. In a quiet but authoritative French voice asks if you have had a chance to check out the wine list. You carefully open it to the bubbles section. You can't believe it; not only do you spy they have your favorite Champagne, but it a vintage you've only heard about in Wine Spectator. With childlike enthusiasm, you order the Taittinger: Comtes de Champagne Blanc de Blancs, 2007 vintage. Smiling to yourself as you said it perfectly! He says, "Magnificent choice Monsieur," and disappears.

You and your date are taking in the entire dreamy scene. She is looking lovingly into your eyes. She takes her napkin and wipes a tiny bit of crumb from the corner of your mouth.

You are holding hands, playing footsie under the table. She's running her foot up ever so slightly up your pant leg. Your waiter returns pretending not to notice with one of those fancy-schmancy standalone table side wine stands. Your incredible selection is resting inside the ice-filled chrome bucket.

Your waiter has procured two stunning Cristal D'Arques Flutes. Dappled sunlight is creating a rainbow on the table from those exquisite glasses.

He expertly pops the formerly dusty bottle and serves you a teaser amount with one hand for you to sample. Taittinger's Juggernaut release tickles your nose as you savor the complexity that the chalky soil made that it was grown in not far from here. You admire its golden color replete with a light floral bouquet. Tiny perfectly formed bubbles are frantically raging now. You slowly savor this nectar of the gods which lingers on your palate like a great Cuban cigar. Spicy, yet delicate, delectable scintillating and supremely satisfying. Eat your heart out Napoleon Bonaparte, you laugh inside. It's the finest Champagne you can ever remember tasting. You nod with astonishing approval. Two thumbs up!! He then pours your date a healthy glass then refills yours fully.

He bids you both "À votre santé." Cheers in French. Your handmade glasses create a beautiful tone as they kiss each other; only real crystal can produce that pitch. As you clank them together, toasting your relationship; you simultaneously move your faces closer to steal a quick kiss. Onlookers from other tables are smiling.

A scene from the movie "When Harry Met Sally" runs through your mind.

Reading that, how did it make you feel? Did it put you into a romantic mood? The great thing about romance is that it doesn't have to resemble a cheesy Hallmark film to be amazing.

Note to the men reading this. Take romance seriously.

It's the glue that binds memories, happy times, and solidifies relationships.

Your job is to make her feel as she's never felt before. News flash, it takes creativity. If we don't take care of the romantic side of our relationships, it can easily change into one of passion that fizzled into mere convenience.

No way around it, lasting relationships take work.

Sadly, others just don't or won't do the work required to keep the relationship alive and thriving.

Remember that in the beginning, romantic gestures most likely took your relationship well past the friendship stage.

There is no magic potion for permanent relationships, I believe that one of the secrets of a true and lasting relationship is bringing out all the qualities that your partner possesses, forgetting each other flaws and offering understanding, support, and unconditional love in most any situation.

People with whom I have discussed the topic of intimacy generally gravitate towards the physical aspect of such. Romance is another word that often comes up as well as a mental connection.

I'd suggest that real intimacy is only partially physical. The combination of mental and emotional magnifies the physical. It stems from mutual openness. It can happen by allowing the other to see your vulnerabilities. This requires a tremendous amount of trust. Scary perhaps however the reward is incredible.

When one connects with someone deeply, it's as if each other can see into one another's being. They've become intertwined. Some people refer to this as meeting their Soul Mate.

Every relationship is a two-way street. A thriving one is based on love, sincerity, and above all, making each other feel how important and beloved they are.

A romantic relationship is something which many of us desire; yet eludes some. The simple truth is that if you want more romance out of yours, you must be a willing and active participant; thereby stoking the loving passionate fires in the hearts of our partners.

Sadly, passion is fleeting for many, it tends to fizzle out after the couple passes out of the NRE- New Relationship Energy excitement phase into the mundane of everyday life.

Don't fall prey to this downward spiral of romantic mediocrity. Small, thoughtful daily gestures can keep our partners longing and hungry for more, resulting in happy reciprocation. Knowing your partner's specific "Love Language" makes this a snap!

When we do romantic things we keep our relationship fresh and exciting, thereby creating fond memories that last a lifetime.

The dictionary states that "Romance" is a feeling of excitement and mystery associated with love. Much wisdom lies therein.

I often wonder why men become so damned complacent after they get married or have been in an LTR? They probably worked hard in the beginning to snare their prize. Back in the day when they were trying to woo their Beloved, it was bringing flowers and taking them to nice restaurants. Why did they stop? Boredom, complacency, familiarity, laziness? Only they can answer that question.

Word to the wise is to continue to grow your romance; again this takes effort, not a lot of money.

Let's take a quick look at the seven types of love. The following theory is based on renowned Psychologist Robert J Sternberg's *Triangular Theory of Love* which he first shared back in 1985 at Yale University. His treatise is fairly straight forward, starting with the three main components. Sternberg believed that in the heart of most human relationships lie passion, commitment, and intimacy.

Taken individually, these components form the three simplest forms of love – passion alone brings infatuation, intimacy alone equals liking, and commitment alone means empty love. Here's his theory in a nutshell, We have Infatuation=Passion. Next "Liking"=Intimacy. Then Empty Love=Commitment. Next is Fatuous

Love=Commitment and Passion. On to this chapter's contents; Romantic Love=Passion and Intimacy, moving on to Companionate Love=Intimacy and Commitment and finally, Consummate Love= Passion, Intimacy, and Commitment.

I won't go into the minutiae of his brilliant theory as it can be readily looked up online. My purpose rather is to give the reader a look at romance with a scientific mind. Romance has little to do with becoming a scientist; much like a chemist looking to create new compounds by combining atoms of their constituent elements by ionic bonds or by covalent bonds. In other words they mix various chemicals to create new ones.

Like the chemist, today's Romantic Warrior looks for new ways to spice up their relationship. Creating exciting ways to enhance your relationship will do wonders for you both.

For years, I heard that romance is the number one feeling which people desire above all else, in fact they chase after it. I never liked that assumption; some people do, some do not. However, doing so can make your significant other feel a deeper connection with you.

It is doing those little things without telling them that make your partner feel loved and cherished by you. Things that may surprise you; mentioning the day you met or anniversary to friends, remembering to put the toilet seat down, replacing empty toilet paper rolls, taking out the trash all without being reminded or hounded to do so. Not leaving your clothes on the floor. Picking up after yourself, not leaving a mess for her to have to deal with.

Consider these 'house rules,' to save countless hours of argument.

If you open it…close it.

If you drop it…pick it up.

If you take it out…put it back.

If you make a mess…clean it up.

It's my firm belief that romance is a necessary component and ought to be a daily occurrence in our lives. Again, knowing your partner's specific love language takes the guesswork out of the equation. The secret is that there are no secrets to being romantic, just making the effort without being nudged to do so is the key.

Welcome to Basecamp Romeo; a place where fellow Romantic Warriors find respite and ways to fire up their relationships.

Here are a few ideas to consider adding more romance to your relationship.

Note, I have written these from my own male perspective but apply equally each way.

Tell her daily how much you love her; do so with conviction and nonchalantly.

Tell her she's beautiful and you'd marry her again in a heartbeat.

After you get married or have been together for a long period, continue having date nights.

Put little notes in places she is bound to see them.

When talking to her, PAY ATTENTION. Put your cell phone down, turn off Sports Center, put down the remote, pause your computer game, put the controller down (It isn't going anywhere), and listen to them. Really listen.

Surprise her with a deep romantic hug when she walks into the room followed by a kiss the way you did when you first met; full-on, no holds barred. Knock her off their feet. Make her weak in the knees.

Pucker up, Buttercup.

Keep surprising her; be spontaneous! Tell her you've got something special in mind that you think she will love and then do it.

Do the unexpected, Blow her mind. Be a "Man of Mystery".

Flirt with her. Create pet names of affection between you.

Hold the door for her. Stand up when she gets up from the table.

Demonstrate classy public displays of affection.

Thank her when you notice she does something that she said she would work on. You in turn do your part and live up to your word about also doing the things you agreed to. Such as things she did that you might normally take care of like cutting the lawn.

Hold hands in a public place.

Show her that chivalry is still alive and well in your house.

Don't be afraid to be vulnerable with her, wear your heart on your sleeve. Let her see your tender, compassionate side. Don't be afraid to cry in front of her either. Suppressing your hurt always seeks expression in other areas of your life.

Have her favorite flowers delivered to her work with a romantic card. She will be the envy of the office.

Take a ride in your car, find a secluded spot, and make out.

Tug lightly on her hair.

If she is physically in pain or sore, offer to run a bath for her or a nice massage. Foot rubs rock!! Don't rush through it just to get it done.

Offer to do her chores which she normally does if she's running late or is not feeling well. A caring relationship strives to be 50/50 split; however, sometimes it may be 40/60 and so on. Don't keep score on what you did. She will notice.

Celebrate her small successes as they happen.

Try new things weekly, such as new board games, different types of movies, make meals together, things you've never had before, or bring home a new type of food you've never tried before from a restaurant.

Call her during the day just to say "Hi, how's your day going?" Or send her sexy texts. Ask her, "What are you wearing?"

Make friends with other couples that you both like to hang out with.

The possibilities are endless; one thing I can promise you is that by making the effort can transform a lackluster relationship into a vibrant and more fulfilling one.

Try it for yourself, what have you got to lose?

What is your fantasy date? Experience it in your vivid imagination with all of your senses on board.

What kind of pleasure and play would you like to experience with that special someone?

Can you come up with a love list that you can tap into to make the relationship fun and fresh?

CHAPTER 21:

HOW TO LIVE HAPPILY WITH ANOTHER PERSON

"You know you're in love when you can't fall asleep because reality is finally better than your dreams."
~ Dr. Seuss

The esteemed Dr. David Viscott wrote a bestselling book called; *How To Live With Another Person.* Wonderfully written, poignant, and helpful. In the book he discussed step by step; how to set goals for yourself and your relationship.

How to draw up an agreement with your partner and live by it. How to conduct a good argument and avoid a destructive fight. How to recognize the little things that can either pull two people apart or draw them together more closely. What to do when partners change. How to understand and deal with sexual infidelity. How to tell if your relationship is in trouble and how to save it.

I highly recommend it. I loved it as much as "Language of the feelings." I think it marries with this chapter quite well.

Re-reading Dr. Viscott's classic, made me ponder ways that work for Michelle and me.

These are in no particular order.

We have mutual respect and never force our ideas on each other.

We have learned how to communicate effectively without yelling. We are mindful and present choosing our words and how we speak and relate to each other. We don't need to win every argument; when we have opposing points of view, to diminish a potential conflict we don't tell each other they are wrong. We simply can agree to disagree and let it go; by doing this we don't hold underlying or any residual anger towards each other.

Where possible we address things as they come up ASAP; by doing so, these things can be talked rationally about and not left to fester, escalate, and create even more issues. Afterward we resolve not to bring it up again as long as it doesn't happen again.

Learning to keep my mouth shut has been a Godsend. We never shame nor purposely embarrass the other in front of our friends or family.

Both of us realize being happy is more important than being right. We are mindful of the beauty we each bring into our relationship. We don't need to compete for each other's affection. We both contribute equally, emotionally, physically, and financially where possible. We both do our fair share of the household duties and chores without having to ask the other. We take turns watching each other's movies, documentaries, and listening to their favorite music.

Neither of us air our dirty laundry in public or on social media, these are the issues that only concern us. We have no time for "one-upmanship." We can laugh at ourselves when appropriate, we cry together, both in happy and sad times. We have grown comfortable with ourselves and our relationship never having to prove to strangers just how "totally bitchin" we are. We already know that fact, just kidding. We prefer harmony over drama, we realize how damaging playing those infantile, childish games are. We strive daily for balance and equanimity.

I will close this chapter with the following question I posed to the focus group.

For those of you in an LTR, (Long Term Relationship)

What's your secret? What's that one thing you do to keep your marriage or relationship fresh and exciting?

Here are a few of their answers.

"Over time I have come to believe that expecting someone to fulfill your expectations is a doomed endeavor. Better to just relish the areas where you and your S.O. come together and build on those. There are times when high expectations will lead to a different time's anger and/or frustrations."

"Tom, it may not be very exciting or spontaneous but speaking after 30+ years, it's all about the commitment; the commitment to your significant other, your children, and God."

"Communication! You have to talk to each other about everything, don't hold back. Easier said than done! 43 years this May 7th."

"Early in our relationship, we saw a therapist who told us that we would succeed because we had our own language. It is the way in which we speak to each other. I've never forgotten it and it's so true, even now, 20 years later." "Put the other person first and learn to use your words for what you need and how you feel."

"Victoria's Secret"

"This is my longest relationship ever, almost eight years now. I would say to have a happy, healthy, long term relationship, you need to, first of all, be happy with yourself; love yourself, know your worth and not ever settle for less. In my younger years I didn't have self-love or know what I deserve. Finding my forever love at 40, I do things so much differently. I practice patience, understanding, respect his own individuality, value his friendship, have 100% trust, NO YELLING. We disagree calmly, while we may not completely agree with each other's opinion, we listen to each other, and again respect our differences. We laugh together, we cry together, we go through challenges together, United as a team! Always keeping things fresh like a coffee date, or movie night with popcorn, does not have to be fancy, but it's so important to always Date your Mate."

My husband Tom and I will be married 45 years next month. The commitment that we made in front of God, family, and friends is huge and has gotten us through any rough patches, and there were many during the child-raising years. Having our parents supporting us and never taking sides was also key. But I think the biggest key for us was that we learned that we didn't need to win every argument, and not everything was worth an argument."

"Honesty, communication, commitment, SENSE OF HUMOUR, forgiveness, weekly date day, finding common interests, keeping your own friends and interests, and doing things separately as well as together. Reminding yourself about your partner's good qualities when they're driving you crazy. Remembering why you fell in love with them in the first place. Putting them first, making sacrifices. Looking after yourself and being careful to self-nurture. BALANCE!

Not needing to have the last word. Forgive. Let go. Yes, I put forgive twice! 40 years married, would die for him if I had to."

"A couple that laughs together, stays together."

"Sorry, I'm of NO help! Single for 36 years with only a couple relationships since! But my kitties think I'm amazing in our relationships."

"My husband and I have been together for almost 12 years (July) and married for four as of February. We've never been monogamous. I am mindful of his awesomeness and treat him like the amazing human he is, and he does the same with me. We don't force each other to compete for attention (that would be shitty), but recognizing that one's significant other is rad and has other rad people to love, be loved by and spend time with in addition to one is very motivating to cultivate one's personal awesome."

"Dale and I will be married 12 years on June 21st. We realized that to keep the marriage fresh and new we had to continue to date each other. We try to go on

1-2 dates a month and act like it's our first one. We realize that people tend to change as they grow so we have continued to make it a habit to continue to learn about each other. We try to never take each other for granted and will occasionally buy random gifts for each other just because."

"Your marriage or relationship will NOT be fresh or exciting all the time, that's ok. Are you both committed to being the best YOU first and then the best US next? Are you respectful, honest, and kind? Do you look for ways to help each other? Do you listen attentively (that takes a lot of practice)? After nearly 20 years together I can say we fight well, we deeply respect ourselves and each other, we are willing to do the hard work to communicate through the hard stuff, we are willing to be inconvenienced for each other (not too often though) and we know we care for each other. That, to me, is successful. It's not going to be hot sex and the honeymoon stage forever."

"I just lost my wife of 36 years because I spent five years being a drunk. I say the key is paying close attention, lots of love, romantic gestures."

"Communication, honesty, freedom, respect, forgiveness, support, encouragement, commitment. Openness to trying new ideas and activities, take turns."

"Friendship, kindness, and respect."

"Support the differences and help align and support personal boundaries. I'm a work-a-aholic. So is my husband. We appreciate each other's work ethic but help each other for work/life balance. We are vastly different people but respect each other and sometimes have to over talk things out to get on the same page. But every day and every effort is worth it."

What stories do you have to share about your past or current relationships?

What are/were the best aspects of those partnerships?

What are/were the most challenging?

CHAPTER 22:

KEEPING IT REAL

*"Since the invention of the kiss, there have been only
five kisses that were rated the most passionate,
the most pure. This one left them all behind."*
~ *The Princess Bride*

Is it just me or does it seem to you that too many
formerly good relationships got stale? I've heard stories
from Facebook acquaintances as to what they did when
that happened. Their answers varied and were all over the
map. They ranged from coldness and aloofness by either
partner, to spending more time doing things with friends.
They used other ways to sublimate boredom, feeling
unfulfilled or sadness, such as shopping, gambling,
gaming, drinking, drugging, watching porn, or starting to
troll for other partners on Tinder. Some went into online

chat rooms and many more lascivious activities. Terribly sad methinks that some people would risk their marriage or LTR because it just wasn't fun anymore. Not that their significant other did something abhorrent to them or had an affair, they simply wanted a little excitement. They longed for something new, unknown. Something exciting, perhaps the thought that it was considered taboo or dangerous was a turn on for them, only they knew for sure. The sad truth is that this happens daily. It has been going on in society for many years.

There is so much mistrust, hurt, despair, and pain created when one partner pulls any of that. To piss away something once cared deeply about for a secret tryst boggles my mind. It's so difficult to find someone one feels comfortable with. For me, trying to figure out what's missing and work to improve it rather than start over is the better way to go.

It got me thinking…

What are some ways that keep a relationship FRESH, exciting, and alive? Knowing her love languages will make this easy to do.

I posed that question to the focus group and some delightful suggestions emerged.

I have written this coming from a man's point of view; however, these ideas can work both ways.

Weekly "Date Nights" -Doesn't have to be fancy nor expensive, just one specific day to spend with your mate. No cell phones allowed. This is your time to rekindle and keep the magic in your relationship.

Start flirting again.

Surprise them- Do things you've never done before; show them you still have few tricks up your sleeve.

Keep them guessing- Have fun with this. Do things they never will expect.

Be a person of mystery- There's a difference between withholding important information your mate should know and cool things bout you which you never shared, a particular skill or talent you have.

Blow their mind- Take them to that restaurant they've been dying to try, buy that special gift they've had their eye on, and surprise them with it for no special reason.

Do something outrageous- Wear something LOUD that you normally wouldn't wear, get down on a knee and tell them you'd marry them again.

Do the unexpected- Take them for a ride in the car to share something cool with them.

Be spontaneous- Don't let them know when you've cooked up a special plan. Be sly but fun.

Plan a weekend or weeknight getaway- These can help a relationship charge their emotional juices and rekindle your romance.

Take salsa lessons together.

Take a one-night painting class together.

Hit a comedy club.

Learn how to play an instrument and serenade her.

Go to a karaoke club and dedicate her favorite song to her.

Have chocolate-dipped strawberries delivered to her work or at home.

Leave love notes in her purse, in her car or someplace she will see them.

Send her sexy texts during the day.

Whatever her hobby is, pick up something that she will use.

Bring her an unexpected gift, a piece of jewelry perhaps that you think she would like. Tell her all the reasons she deserves it and mean it.

Find a romantic spot you can drive to and make out like you used to.

"Wine her"- If you aren't that familiar with wines, educate yourself. Take her to a restaurant, do your homework beforehand and study their wine list (go online) When the server comes; ask for the wine list. And order a bottle that your partner likes. While it's impressive to buy the most expensive bottle, the trick here is not having to buy the most expensive bottle on the list, it's to be smart enough to know how to cherry-pick it and find the screaming deal. Pull out all the stops when your bottle comes. Look at the label and make sure it's what you ordered. Have your server pour you a sample, swirl your glass, smell the aromas.

Comment as to the varietal (type) of grape. Where it was grown, the aromas that waft forth from it. Its bouquet and appearance. There are no wrong answers there. Then have your sever pour your date a glass. Savor the moment.

Romance her belly-If you don't cook regularly, surprise her with a home-cooked meal.

Bring her breakfast in bed and dress up like a fancy waiter.

Ask her about her day and PAY ATTENTION to her answers.

Buy tickets for something she has wanted to see/hear

Even if you don't dance well, grab her hand, and ask for this dance, right in your living room or in the front yard, not being concerned about how you look.

227

Get your groove on. Throw caution to the wind. Let your hair down. Let it all hang out.

Bring her dessert in bed as well, you may get a surprise too.

Attend costume parties as a combo, Romeo & Juliet, Bonnie & Clyde, Cleopatra & Marc Antony, Hansel & Gretel, etc.

Dress up for dinner at home. Put on that sport coat. Have candles burning, music on low. Look into her eyes. Tell her you love her.

Wear brand new cologne.

Write a poem and recite it to her.

Bring back chivalry into your life, hold doors for her, stand up as when she leaves or returns to the dinner table. Hold her hand.

Smack her on the butt when she walks by and tell her how beautiful she is.

The possibilities are endless, the point is to do it.

Watch how your relationship re-blossoms.

I will leave you with something I found beautiful that a Facebook follower shared with me.

"I've been married and divorced twice before, now I am in an 8-year relationship that is quite different than my marriages. It is the most beautiful thing which feeds my soul! Knowing that I have a base to return to, a supportive space that is safe and secure allows me to be more adventurous in my development.

Ways to nurture that support include amazingly simple things for us. We make eye contact whenever possible when we talk.

We put our phones away for 95% or more of the time we are together. We listen for what matters to the other and in some way relate to it. I once mentioned something in passing and a month or so later we were with friends and he mentioned that accomplishment of mine but with such tenderness and pride. We aren't in a typical relationship and we don't live in the same town, but we make sure that the time we do get to spend together matters. It's the only relationship I've ever been in where I truly have never questioned how much I am loved, and he says he hasn't either. I also think that because of how our relationship has evolved that we truly and completely want what is best for each other. What is beautiful is that we don't have an attachment to what that looks like. He trusts me completely to find my way and I feel the same. We celebrate when those roads meet and know that when they diverge again we will find our way back again. It's been a beautiful journey so far."

Her story melted my heart.

In closing, if you're blessed enough to be in a loving, committed relationship you know how important it is to keep it fresh. Sadly, many times after the initial excitement and newness wears off, we (men) tend to quit doing those little things that added SPARKS when it was just starting. Word to the wise...CONTINUE doing those little things. These kind actions don't have to cost a lot. Tell her she's beautiful. Be creative. Showing continued appreciation will engender those happy feelings which are usually reciprocated 10-fold. The key is knowing exactly what your loved one's "Love Language" is. Check out the classic *The 5 Love Languages* by Dr. Gary Chapman for the skinny. By demonstrating these small daily gestures, you will be rewarded many times over with a happier mate; more importantly, you will love how it makes you feel. Try it and let me know how it transforms your relationship.

Has your relationship gotten a little stale?

What creative ideas do you have to enliven it?

Do you realize that each party involved is equally responsible for keeping it fresh?

CHAPTER 23:

LOVE HAS NO EXPIRATION DATE

"There is never a time or place for true love.
It happens accidentally, in a heartbeat,
in a single flashing, throbbing moment."
~ Sarah Dessen

Throughout my research, I have heard countless stories of people finding love in their twilight years. Some thought they'd never experience that feeling; others had many relationships but never felt they found the One.

Others had been looking for love in all the wrong places their entire adult life. Some had been married early on, got divorced or their longtime partner died.

Some said they felt lucky to have found what they called their second or real love late in life. They never gave up hope or quit looking. The point here is that if you are currently looking, open to welcoming your relationship, and don't give up. Keep the faith. It's usually darker before the light of dawn breaks into the day.

Hearing these stories made me ponder people's reasons for seeking a committed relationship at the later stages in life. While their sex drives may have played a part, it seemed to me it was more for wanting companionship. There are many aspects of love. After the initial carnal desires begin to diminish or lessen their amorous calling, the heart continues to beckon to be fulfilled. I was talking with a dear friend the other day. It was near Mother's Day. She sighed and said the last four years had been hard since her mother passed away. She had been fighting cancer. Both she and her mom had come to grips with the inevitable; it was her dad that it hit hardest. They had been married for over 50 years. After her mother died, her father went into a deep depression. He didn't want to remain in the home as it brought up too many memories and the upkeep was more than he wanted to continue, so he opted to move into Assisted Living. My friend was able to visit him daily as he lived fairly close. Her father grew up near the Oregon coast and his son lived there. He had a hankering to move back. My friend helped her dad get his affairs in order and moved him there. Several months after he settled in, she noticed her father seemed happier, she inquired what happened. He shared that he had a girlfriend. She was surprised and somewhat relieved at the same time. His only complaint was the food. Evidentially it was so bad he decided to move back to Portland. This, however, didn't stop this 85 man from making the two hours back and forth from the coast every few days.

Sadly, his lady passed on. He was single again. Within a few months he had another girlfriend. While they haven't married, supposedly they are still a happy couple today.

So where am I going with all this?

Where there are unfulfilled wants and needs, there's desire, and a catalyst. Sprinkle in unrelenting hope, fueled with optimism and you have a driving force. In my friend's case, her belief was her father hated being alone. Some of the people's stories which I briefly touch upon indicated they weren't looking; they were open but weren't actively pursuing a relationship. Love found a way for them and it can happen for you.

Social media has been a blessing for me in that the amount of wonderful online friendships that have developed as a result of my writing and daily postings. While writing this book; I posted one of the questions I used earlier, about what people were looking for in their relationship.

233

What was the one thing they had to have?

One of my wise friends named Rick, sent me a private message after I commented on his answer to my question. I thanked him for his pithy response and complimented him noting there was much wisdom in his answer.

With his permission, I will share what he wrote to me as it sheds wonderful light on this chapter.

He wrote:

"Thank you, Tom. It didn't happen overnight. It's funny how long we allow ourselves to stumble over ourselves to finally see the light. Sometimes I think wisdom is one of our greatest accomplishments and invaluable. I'm glad to see that you are living the dream and sharing it with your beautiful accomplice! It gives an old man like me inspiration to find a trusting lady, not an easy task these days. Unfortunately, today we have to be politically correct and have to role play in different circles. I am from the South, I maintain my respect and while I am used to rendering compliments, sadly many times they have been misinterpreted.

As we get older, a lot of people have gone through many mishaps and relationships. They have a set view of what the next person will be like. I can't believe how many are lonely because of their inhibitions which stand in their own way to take a chance on happiness.

It is so sad and unnecessary for way too many. Lack of trust and conditioned insecurities are a vicious result, the main reason people put up walls and essentially stay in their own bubble. They lock out the world outside of their established perimeters. I have hoped that my "picker's not broken". I will maintain my old fashion values. I've always been the giver in my past relationships, but oh my God, there's too many to accommodate. I finally had to put myself first. It's been an amazing transition. Learning and applying that NO is a full sentence and trusting my gut when necessary.

Thanks for letting me ramble on. I am interested in how your book turns out. All I know about relationships is, I believe that women have the power and rule the roost. They can render us powerless without much effort! The worst part of it is when there are ulterior motives; that we have to be skeptical about what trap does not allow us to get stuck in. Believe me when I express a mystery that I have; not proudly I had a lot of relationships; from being married for 26 years and sleeping with almost 60 women yet I have not yet found the long-term chemistry or compatibility I have sought for the long haul. For men, I'm at the age that companionship is significant. I have optimism that God will provide it in his own time. I don't want to just settle on someone because I'm lonely, it will be a big plate to fill and she's out there. Time is so much more valuable as we age. It creates its own urgency and it takes a lot of patience to not repeat old behaviors. For me, getting laid is easy, but finding a soulmate has been extremely difficult. Communication is number one to me, paralleled with trust is imperative for a solid foundation to begin with. Women are the most unpredictable creatures on this planet. Anybody that believes differently is a fool!

Good luck my friend and I look forward to maybe running into you one of these days. Take care. Rick"

I like Rick's message for several reasons.

He wrote from his heart. He has come to terms with who he is, where he has been, and what he's looking for. He's kept the faith. He set boundaries. He is an eternal yet realistic optimist. He's opened his heart while taking his brain with him. He shares his beliefs that work for him and doesn't appear to attempt to force them on anyone.

My gut feeling tells me his soulmate is out there and eventually they will connect.

Can you be patient, growing into the person you want to be, as you open yourself to late in life love?

Do you have role models for people who find new love with whom to celebrate the next chapters?

What are the benefits and challenges in this type of relationship?

CHAPTER 24:

SO, YOU WANNA BE A MACHO MAN?

"I knew I was different. I thought that I might be gay or something because I couldn't identify with any of the guys at all. None of them liked art or music. They just wanted to fight and get laid. It was many years ago, but it gave me this real hatred for the average American macho male."
~Kurt Cobain

Big shout out to my bestie Michelle, my talented wife. The benefit of having someone's opinion you can trust when writing has been a supreme blessing. She lovingly listened to every chapter that was written, sharing ideas on how to make it better along the way.

Michelle has a keen knack of pointing things out that I miss and things that should be omitted that can help the flow of any given chapter.

Last night, after we both finished working, Michelle and I took the semi-daily tour of our property.

In 2018, we moved from the hustle and bustle of big city life to the slower, calmer paced country, a densely forested nook in the upper rural area of Beavercreek, Oregon. Working farms hide in the open behind the mailboxes and long driveways of the people living there. Their horses, cattle, and goats seem to beckon one to stop by and say hello.

You can see the jewel in Oregon's Cascade crown, her spectacular mountain majesty Mt Hood, which is one of Oregon's main tourist attractions, from our winding country roads. The first time we visited this magnificent, secluded, three-acre, hilltop homestead, dotted with hundreds of mature trees and fauna, brimming with a host of wildlife; mountain lions, black bear, raccoons, skunks, beaver, majestic bald eagles, blue heron, turkey vultures, and numerous indigenous songbirds, we knew immediately we had finally found our dream house. It is a tranquil, meditative welcoming place which I lovingly refer to as "The Zen Gardens" which Michelle has dubbed "Black Squirrel Hallow."

We have a cherished ritual we do mainly during the early spring through late fall, as we look with childlike wonder at the new growth that the seasonal changes nature has provided us.

It allows Michelle and me to flirt, chit chat about our respective days, etc. It's the fun work that healthy couples do daily as part of nurturing their relationships. We had just fed our Koi in the large cement pond and were sitting under our pergola on our trek deck sipping an icy cold brewski.

Michelle's eyes beamed as she had an idea, she suggested the book needed two chapters; one about men, one about women which would include their differences and commonalities.

"Great idea," I said with a sly grin. I was planning to write a combined synopsis dealing with stereotypes, but this seemed like a better way to go.

In these next two chapters, I will attempt to dispel old beliefs that don't hold much merit in today's societal norms, at least not here in the U.S. It seemed to me, many ideas people have about how "REAL men and women" were supposed to behave, act and think were as extinct as *Mammuthus primigenius* a.k.a. the Woolly Mammoth.

For decades I had pondered characteristics of both sexes. I see many of these as outdated generalities,

239

however, they shed light on old mindsets of days gone by that some people still operate out of today in 2020.

In no way is this meant to be a complete list, there are many books already published filled to the brim with this type of information. It's meant to stir and elevate people's consciousness.

Note: Something I always point out in anything I share; is that in no way am I suggesting any of the ideas written ahead are right; they are only right in my way of thinking. Every generality can often be disproven, in that, some people will say: "that's not true for me" and yes, in their case and they'd be correct. (Memes also can fall into this category.) They would fit into the group of people which esteemed bestselling author Malcolm Gladwell so eloquently wrote about which he referred to as Outliers.

Malcom stated: "An outlier is an observation that lies an abnormal distance from other values in a random sample from a population. In a sense, this definition leaves it up to the analyst (or a consensus process) to decide what will be considered abnormal. ... These points are often referred to as outliers."

He refers to these folks as the best and the brightest, the most famous and the most successful. He asks the question: what makes high-achievers different and shares ways they see things differently than most people?

That said, allow me to debunk some long-held stereotypes. For our discussion, we need to examine different examples of stereotyping. I will define my definition of what my research has shown me. Any time one groups races or individuals together and makes a judgment about them without having the faintest clue about them, would be a good example of a stereotype. My research concluded that stereotypes are widely held, simplified, and essentialist beliefs about a specific group, man, or woman in our case. Groups are generally stereotyped based on their sex, gender identity, ethnicity and race, nationality, age, socioeconomic status, language, how they look, and so forth. Stereotypes are deeply embedded within social institutions.

It seems to me that practically every culture on Earth has some kind of stereotypical beliefs.

Early famous researchers Katz and Braly published one of the first documented reports on Racial Stereotyping back in 1933 in which 100 Princeton University students were asked to indicate the traits most characteristic of ten different social groups from a list of 84 words. Students displayed a high level of agreement about the traits of certain racial and ethnic groups. Their conclusion was that ethnic stereotypes were wide spread. The bottom line to be remembered is that stereotyping is not only hurtful, it is also wrong. Period.

Let's start with us men.

Men are not to show their feelings- Ha, this one is comical. Today's refined man has embraced both his dark and light nature as well as the masculine and feminine aspects of his persona. No judgment, just acceptance is all. If that is your goal. here are a few great points to become that fully integrated man.

Be Open to Your Vulnerabilities, Physical, Social, Economic, and Attitudinal.

Know the difference between your perceived weaknesses and your vulnerabilities. Weakness can be defined as lacking strength where vulnerability is being susceptible to injury.

True acceptance comes from being truly vulnerable.

Deeper intimacy happens as follows:

Communication requires rigorous honesty

> Which leads to understanding

> > Which leads to trust

> > > Which generates deeper
> > > intimate loving

Men Rule the roost- Maybe in the early part of the last century.

Men are in control and they alone are the backbone of society. No longer true. Today, women are working in places of power and decision making. For decades they have continued climbing the rungs of power. They are heads of state, run corporations, and heavily influence media.

Men don't change their baby's dirty diapers. -Men who value their relationship contribute in all ways, such as feeding, bathing, and reading to their children. The evolved man knows these types of actions create deeper bonds with their child as well as gaining deeper respect and trust from their partners.

Real men don't eat quiche. The person who said that had no idea how delicious it is. For those who aren't old enough to remember, *Real Men Don't Eat Quiche: A Guidebook To All That Is Truly Masculine* written by Robert Feirstein is a spoof on stereotypical masculinity. It was published in the 1980s and sadly, some still don't see the humor in it.

Men are the key decision-makers in every household.- In today's complex society, all decisions are made together. This makes for a win-win in their relationship.

Men are the primary breadwinners.- Today's working women contribute equally or as much as they can afford to the household.

Men believe women are subservient to men.- Go ahead and try to lay that one on my wife.

Men are the superior rational thinkers.-While women tend to be more emotionally centered, this in no way diminishes their cognitive abilities to reason as well or better than men. Everyone is different in this department.

Men rule their wives.- Not even gonna go there.

Men discipline the children.- Today, this duty is shared, or the decision is made who will be the good cop and who will be the bad cop.

Fathers know best.- Robert Young was a perfect on-screen TV dad. Sadly, reality today is far from what the screenwriter of yesteryear wrote into every episode. They were someone else's fantasy.

Men don't do household chores, they work on cars and do the yard work, women clean the house, do the laundry, and pick up after the husband.- Today's good couple split the chores and decide who will do what. They make compromises and strive to keep it fair, as well as not forcing them to have their mate do something they hate. Keep in mind that if you make a mess, it is your job to clean up after yourself, not your partner's.

Men have earned the right to be messy. This works both ways. Nothing can drive me as crazy as an unorganized, dirty, messy domicile.

Men are strong and do all the work.- If the man is physically stronger, then perhaps he would do some of the heavy-duty jobs around the house that the woman may not be able to perform. There are certainly women who have more strength and stamina than men.

Men do a far better job than women.-This man is never getting laid.

Men who spend too much time on the computer or read are geeks. Today's man wears multiple hats. It's good to know your way around the computer and not just for gaming; it's equally good to be filling your mind with good food for thought that expands your previous thinking.

Effeminate men are all gay; homosexuality is wrong, immoral, and an abomination.- I am disappointed and surprised that in 2020, we haven't moved on from homophobic bias. People are people regardless of their gender identities or sexual preferences.

Whose business is it anyway what consenting adults do in the privacy of their own home as long as they aren't hurting anyone? People would do better to mind their own business and quit trying to force their morality on others. The world would be a better place.

My wife strongly suggested that I leave out negative ones about other cultures.

Just a few closing points here before moving on to the female stereotyping chapter.

Men and women are wired differently. Both bring different strengths and weaknesses to the table because of that fact; both bring value to their relationship. It seems to me, men are easier to figure out, but what do I know? I can tell you that we are not mind readers. We hate that old game some women lay on us, "We'll you should know that by now".

News Flash, we don't.

Most men know their basic feelings, when they're hungry, horny, sleepy, etc. If you want something, TELL THEM. Please do this… Please avoid that. Tactful honesty goes a long way. If there are certain things you want, show us how you like it.

If we respect you, we will go out of our way to please you. If you feel uncomfortable telling us what you want, you may want to do personal work in that area or perhaps you're with the wrong person.

In closing, the intelligent man realizes that his woman is his best friend. When she sees things differently, he is wise enough not to confuse disagreement with disloyalty. He instinctively knows that she is not in competition with him; ultimately she has his best interests in mind. With her velvet hand, she helps him grow emotionally and spiritually. Her special gifts nurture and revitalize his inner being. He's grateful for this and not ashamed nor embarrassed to tell her that.

Advice to guys, become the intelligent man.

What were you taught about what it means to be a man?

What were you taught about what it means to be a woman?

What myth-busting would you like to do?

CHAPTER 25:

"MICHELLE, THE LIGHT OF MY LIFE"

"For some people, the point of no return begins at the very moment their souls become aware of each other's existence."
~ C. JoyBell C

I had always hoped that after my divorce I would find someone I was romantically attracted to. This time I wanted to marry for love rather than money, obligation or not to avoid being alone.

I met Michelle at "Music Monday" a fundraiser which I held on my property to benefit PAWS Animal Shelter, a local nonprofit that caters to cats. I've been helping PAWS raise donations for about 20 years.

Michelle had been volunteering there for close to a decade and yet our paths never crossed.

These fundraisers I spearhead take many months to plan. Having lived here in Portland, Oregon for 25 years, I am blessed to have connected with many fantastic local musicians who agree to come and play to help this worthy cause. Many of the insurance agents I make sales calls on also donate neat items that we raffle off during these events.

My great friend Noho Marchesi who owns several Hawaiian restaurants generously donated all the foods. These gatherings are fun! I hold then semiannually during August when the possibility of rain is slim. The weather was perfect. I had no idea at the time, just how perfectly the day itself would unfold.

The early evening orange sun peeked through the canopy of the 100-year-old Douglas firs that dotted my back yard which I call "The Zen Gardens." The combined aroma of the hibiscus flowers that graced the property and lemon citronella candles on the tables wafted over the grounds creating a tropical feeling. This year, everything had fallen into place with very few hiccups. I'm guessing there were well over 150 happy people in attendance.

I had finally a chance to take a deep breath and check out the crowd enjoying the melodious sounds of acclaimed indie rocker Pete Krebs (who was killing it).

My youngest daughter Kelsey happened to be standing next to me. That's when I saw her. Michelle's beautiful face beamed, she smiled as she meandered down the pea gravel path to find the PAWS donation table. It was like everything went into slow motion.

She looked angelic. Her long silky black hair gently bounced as she glided into her chair. I suddenly felt a poke against my ribcage from Kelsey who whispered, "Dad, you're staring at that woman." Luckily, she hadn't noticed. Perhaps secretly I wanted her to. And yes, I indeed was staring at that vision of loveliness. I felt there was something incredibly special about her. I had to meet her.

About an hour later I got the chance when she was filling her wine glass near the cooler. My heart melted when she looked into my eyes. Hers were big and brown and exuded kindness and compassion.

My palms were sweating, and my throat was feeling tight. I still managed to make small talk with her. Her voice was as sweet as honey. Now I was really smitten.

When she left, I made a beeline to her friends to inquire whether she was single. I was quickly shot down and heard that she, in fact, was involved in a long-distance relationship. I heard the Pac-Man dying in my mind as I realized I wouldn't be talking to her anytime soon. My rule was that I never got involved with a woman who's seeing someone else as I would hate it if someone did that to me.

Meeting Michelle that first time revived my belief and gave me hope that there still were amazing women out there, simply our timing wasn't right. Fast forward to the following Spring. I had a guardian angel, an ace up my sleeve, yet didn't know it. Kele, a woman who volunteered at PAWS knew Michelle had recently become single and went to work playing matchmaker.

Over several months, she worked her magic and finally convinced Michelle to reach out to me. Michelle added me on Facebook and sent me a text message and mentioned that she had downloaded my first book.

Before I knew it, we went on our initial date. Magic happens when two compatible souls collide. Our first kiss felt like an electric current surged through my body. My knees felt weak. I couldn't wait to see her again.

Soon we were texting and hanging out quite frequently. Shortly after that, I made it official and asked her to be my girlfriend. She agreed.

Everything was going splendidly…or so I believed. Sadly, what transpired just a few short weeks later nearly drove her away from me for good.

If you know me, you will likely agree that I'm pretty intense. I have boundless energy, am overly enthusiastic and demonstrative. I'm headstrong and I am not for everyone. I am constantly on the go. I speak loudly, eat fast, and move quickly. I am super driven; when I see something I want, I go for it, sometimes throwing caution to the wind. This is something I have done my entire life; that by now I should think about more carefully about when making decisions. I like entertaining and hosting gaggles of people. My actions were giving Michelle second thoughts as she is much more reserved than I am.

I was making plans for her to meet a ton of my friends and do many things without consulting her. I made the mistake of not considering her feelings and did not consider that she does not have my energy levels, my GO, GO, GO, take no prisoner's attitude.

The final straw came when I was hosting a backyard BBQ for my oldest daughter Caitlin. There were about 25 people who showed up. Michelle prefers smaller get-togethers and wasn't feeling well. I was oblivious to this, making sure all my guests were having a grand old time. No glass was ever left unfilled.

I assumed she liked big-to-dos as much as I did. She let me know that she was leaving, and as I walked her to her car, I could feel in my gut that something was terribly wrong. We hardly spoke a word on that long, lonely, dismal trek. I told her I felt alone. She coldly said, "What would your book tell you, Tom?

I felt terrible. I was hurt and befuddled. Wasn't sure at that point what I did. I watched mournfully as she drove away. My heart sank. This was on a Thursday. I didn't hear from her until Saturday; in a quick nonchalant text, which didn't sit well with me. Those days with no contact offered many hours to contemplate what went wrong. The moment of truth finally came out; she needed a break from me and that I wasn't considering her needs, wishes, and desires.

Up to this point, my life's motto has been "Far better to be alone than to wish I were." Those last couple of days had seemed painfully long. I was feeling angry and alone. My Anger Dragon had taken control. Sadly, I allowed it to. Sometimes we react in a moment of anger which had we taken the time to really ponder the situation we'd have chosen differently.

That bitter time I was choosing ego over the long-term the benefit of a loving relationship. I decided Michelle and I were finished. I logically chalked up all the nice things I had done for her and determined I didn't deserve the cold shoulder from her, right then and there, I chose to be "right" rather than "happy".

I crafted a beautiful, well-written "Dear John" letter to Michelle. breaking up with her. It's usually easier being the one who dumps as opposed to the opposite.

It wasn't a mean letter; I just voiced my one-sided "Logical" version of the story. I gave her all the reasons I was unhappy and that I hoped we could remain friends. I sent it to her unapologetically. About four hours later, what arrived was the nicest email from Michelle that I had ever received upon breaking up with someone. It blew me away to have had such an experience under those circumstances.

Her kindness didn't sit well with me either. How dare she be so compassionate towards me? I'm the Zen Master after all. For several days of deep thought of what I did, feeling like an idiot full of remorse and self-loathing, I realized what a buffoon I had been. I took some courage to muster the energy to send her a text telling her I missed her. She responded almost immediately saying she missed me too which melted my heart.

That was four months before we got married. I share this story for many reasons. First, that people will hopefully learn from my foolhardiness and think before they act. Too many relationships are cut short by one's ego and lack of communication. Some will choose to be happy over being right. People are different and have their own comfort levels and speed at which they process. Even though Michelle and I were at opposite ends of the speed spectrum, we have learned to meet in the middle.

It recently dawned on me that had I not learned how to tame my inner Anger Dragon and gone through my past healing work I would not have been ready to have Michelle in my life.

Even if she had somehow shown up, it is probable that I wouldn't have had the emotional maturity to have been able to sustain any type of healthy lasting relationship with her or anyone else for that matter.

Michelle and I each realized that we both had fears that arose in us as we got to know each other on deeper levels. This is quite common amongst many people, especially for those of us who've been married before or have not experienced a long-term loving relationship. She is grateful that I accept her as she is; recognizing that she is someone with a completely different approach to living than I have. Communicating with her in a non-judgmental, compassionate manner rather than in an angry or controlling way, made her feel safe enough to want to learn more about responding vs. reacting towards things as I had learned to do.

My new approach to loving communication helped Michelle to be far more open to compromise, meeting me halfway with a loving and positive attitude. What was the secret that helped us move through? The answer may surprise you because it's so straightforward. We had long, deep, honest, heart to heart talks about what scared us. We held nothing back. We listened completely to the other without interrupting or judging. We bared our souls to each other knowing the other could use these words against us when we were angry, however, we knew we wanted to make it work and did it anyway. Not easy but rewarding and necessary if you're going to make your relationship last.

People have asked me how I did it. How did I attract such a loving partner into my life considering the last 10 years since my divorce I hardly dated anyone while dealing with my lingering anger issues?

I've pondered that question deeply and have come up with the following reasons:

- I was ready for a loving relationship.

- I knew exactly what I was looking for. I was seeking someone who matched me on most levels.

- I had worked on the areas of my life which caused me problems in my first marriage. I took ownership of all of them and made slow, daily progress in correcting them.

- I gave up the idea of the "perfect woman" and instead sought out one who was perfect for me.

- I continue to work on our marriage daily, doing the things I had done initially during our courtship that pleased her.

- I give her space and never attempt to control her.

- I respect her opinions and ideas even when they differ from my own.

- I take time every day to have meaningful conversations with her about her day and feelings.

- I gave myself the love which I had never allowed myself to experience. As the old saying goes, we generally receive the love we believe we are deserving of.

- I finally forgave myself for my past and vowed I had gleaned the lessons I needed to heal, grow, and move on.

- I've deep-sixed my perfectionistic past behaviors choosing to be happy than having to have everything always exact. For example, I'm self-proclaimed OCD enhanced "Neat Freak" and Michelle is way more lax and easy going. She doesn't worry if things aren't totally organized.

- I have cured myself of the perfection trap by realizing it is far better to be with the woman of your dreams than to be alone in a sterile house.

- We both snore. When she wakes me up, instead of getting angry I am happy to know my soul mate is home with me in our warm bed.

- When I find Michelle's hair in the drain, I remind myself how lucky I am that my beautiful wife has gorgeous, long, shiny hair.

- When I see cat hair all over the carpet, I no longer freak out and have a "hissy fit." I simply get out the vacuum and give thanks for all of my nine amazing felines. The list goes on… the important thing to remember about my journey is the bigger picture.

- The most important things that truly matter in my life is being a Hope Broker thereby creating joy in others' lives, as well as inner peace, good health, a roof over my head, food on the table, having someone to love, having a job that I love to do and a myriad of things to look forward to.

I'm incredibly happier these days since marrying my best friend.

In closing, I will leave you with a poem my friend Tim Sproul wrote for our wedding called:

"THIS LIGHT ACROSS THE RIVER"

He wondered if that someday

would ever come.

And it did on a magical Music

Monday in Tom's backyard.

It arrived with friends and rock n

roll and exceptionally large servings of

Hawaiian pulled pork.

Oh, he wasn't looking, but he found

a gift of a sudden smile, vanishing

and then returning in the house of

his imagination by the minute.

It began when she sent him a message —

first with her eyes from behind

a glass of Cabernet

and he fell into the light of those jewels

so much so that his daughter Kelsey

had to poke him in the ribs

to keep from staring too hard.

But that's okay, that's Tom

and Tom brings his love strong.

She was there as a volunteer for

PAWS, the animal shelter,

and soon this animal couldn't

keep his paws off her.

But before that, there's got to be hello.

But Tom's a host with more than the most,

with a boyish wonder for friendship and

laughs, a man with a golden heart

and an impeccably green lawn.

He couldn't sit still until everyone

had a healthy plate of food,

a good drink and smiles beaming like light

through those backyard Doug firs.

But he did settle into a feeling for Michelle,

her kindness, volunteering for

the same animal shelter

as he did for a decade.

And yet, somehow they'd never met.

So during his daily meditations of

friendships and high fives,

Tom's feelings grew stronger, a

surround sound love in stereo.

And he cranked it to eleven.

And her, an osprey's glide across

the river to West Linn

would find Michelle throwing wine

parties, painting parties,

making drinks and making dreams

parties, hair parties--

two separate social butterflies

now unknowingly

dancing toward each other.

Sometimes, she wondered, would she

forever be a single crazy cat lady?

And he wondered, would he forever

be a single crazy cat lady?

After a decade of soloing in his

castle of rescued cats

like a suburban Jimmy Page wielding

barbecue tongs as his air guitar,

Tom kept playing that music, that

language of love he spoke daily,

if not on the phone, or in email messages,

then in his love for his garden, his

daughters and, those cats,

all of it dialed in for the woman who

would make his house their home,

her cats their cats—Fisher, Gizmo,

Ichiro, Sylvester, Quincy,

Emma, Kismet, Lily and

Perseus. That's right.

As she poured over his book,

The Department of Zenitation,

he was pouring an openhearted

joy to friends

like those frozen shots of a Russian

vodka, no one could pronounce.

But Tom was fluent in the language

of love blooming for Michelle.

The more she read Tom's book,

the more Michelle started to write

her own story of their love.

And Tom fell hard—there was no half-baked

heart from Mr. Tommy Z.

And so if he did come on a little too strong,

it was in those measured months

when they stepped back,

they found a new rhythm, a

path to a deeper love,

true and now the stories they string together

like those mini-Eiffel Tower lights

framing their living room.

And so, love is music they play

together—through doubt,

through the generosity of time and

faith and just letting it happen,

from that 4th of July first date to

the right here, right now,

alight with colors like that stone

path framed with flowers

leading to the house of his heart.

That distance, this light across

the river, across decades

—she in her cozy cottage, he in

his castle of rescued cats,

now come together.

It's a patience painted with a passion

that says, "let's do this.

Mr. Tim Sproul is an acclaimed creative director and poet, the author of *How to Leave Your Hometown for Good* and *Newported, A Poetic Field Guide to the Pacific Coast.*

Tim lives in Milwaukie, Oregon.

What is the love story you would tell about the way you and a partner met?

How are the two of you similar?

Do you believe that like attracts like or opposites attract?

CHAPTER 26:

TOXIC RELATIONSHIPS 101

*"If you treat me like an option, I'll leave you
like a choice. Treat me like a game,
and I'll show you how it's played."*
~Author Unknown

After my divorce, I grabbed my old emotional swim
trunks and quickly jumped back into the dating pool. It
had been 15 years and I was rustier than a barn
doornail. My childlike enthusiasm overpowered my
mind with blind faith, exuberance, and excitement.
My entire body tingled like a little boy on Christmas
morning staring at all those beautifully wrapped
presents my mother spent hours wrapping. I gushed
when I thought I had found "The One", a potential
long-term partner. It blinded me to much of the

bullshit I had previously experienced. The author Steve Mariboli reminds us that "Sometimes you just have to play the role of the fool to fool the fool who thinks they are fooling you."

I vowed never again to allow the MIND GAMES that I reluctantly had accepted while dating. I would not merely be tolerated in any relationship; I would be celebrated this time. Truth be told, I too was guilty of doing the things which I hated when people did them to me. Michelle also put up with her ex-boyfriends "Gaslighting" because in her earlier days, she lacked self-esteem and emotional intelligence to stand up to them. She settled for average, thinking that was her lot in life. Had she given herself the love she was seeking, she would have kicked those loser ass hats to the curb post haste. Like other quality women, treat her with the respect and love which she deserves, and she'll warm your home, mistreat her and she'll burn it to the ground. Those immature little boys had no idea they had a Queen in their hand and misplayed their cards. Michelle vowed after that to walk away immediately from anyone who didn't see her worth, didn't respect her or cheated on her. For a better part of a decade, she worked on herself. She wasn't actively looking as she believed she eventually would find her King.

Stoicism is one of the games I played. In my younger days, I believed not sharing my true feelings made me appear strong. A manly man who practices stoicism, hiding your feelings- "Acting the Tough Guy" never fools anyone. Having worn the mask, when I see that persona demonstrated, it tells me there's a man who hasn't come to terms with who he is and obliviously ignorant concerning his emotional state.

He may need help but is too proud to ask. He may be seeking understanding, perhaps he simply just wants a friendly, compassionate listener, but he's afraid someone will think him weak for asking for it. Acting like things don't hurt you is disingenuous at best. Any pain or hurt we bury will always be there eventually seeking expression. It will manifest itself in future relationships.

Word to the wise: address any haunting issues. They don't magically disappear. The brave person is willing to admit when they are hurting or what is bothering them. Sharing one's vulnerabilities helps heal the pain and turns it into fuel. It gives that person renewed vigor and hope.

I like the quote attributed to Britney Spears, "Mind games do not make me believe you are mysterious or interesting. Mind games do make me believe you are a waste of my energy and a waste of my time."

I've compiled a list of some game playing found in toxic relationships; to my chagrin, I too was guilty of playing some of them. Each one leads to disharmony in a relationship. They wear away at the foundation and erode trust. Although some actions people take are done because of unconscious patterns, others are willful and intentionally sabotaging.

Being mindful of these traps is valuable; your awareness can assist your relationships to thrive rather than deconstructing.

Here are a few warning signs.

Controlling people- Some game players are master manipulators. Each having their selfish agenda for doing so; reasons stemming from their low self-esteem, insecurity, narcissism, self-centeredness, and dominance. They shrewdly micromanage your life; telling you what to do, who you can see, what to wear, etc. Additionally, they may try to pressure you to do things you don't want to.

They generally don't take "no" for an answer and they use threats, ultimatums, or withhold something they know you want or need. Word to the wise is if you're involved with someone who pulls that stuff, drop them like a bad habit!

Gaslighting- I mentioned this abhorrent behavior in an earlier chapter, but it is well worth repeating. This could have been added to the above point. It's one of the "go to" methods many control freaks use. Gaslighting is a form of psychological manipulation in which a person or a group covertly sows seeds of doubt in a targeted individual, making them question their memory, perception, or judgment, often evoking in them cognitive dissonance and other changes such as low self-esteem.

Some idiot tries this on you....R U N!

Accusing- Accusations can range from saying you're cheating on them or having an affair, or perhaps lying to them about something. Their insecurities play a huge part here, Sometimes it is what they are doing secretly themselves.

The Blame Game- It's always easier to use your faults against you than see their own. In a feeble attempt to conceal their shortcomings, they will point their destructive finger at you, attempting to make you feel like it's your fault. This is a classic symptom of those who fall into addiction. They will often blame you for their troubles and reasons why they do what they do. Addicts find it easy to ignore responsibility for their actions and often use you as their scapegoat. Emotional addicts also fall under this category.

Leading people on when you have no intention of staying in a relationship, merely having one so you don't have to be alone or are waiting for "The One". In other words, keeping "Mr. Right Now while waiting for Mr. Right".

Denial- This is a big one from abusers. Usually, abuse takes place behind closed doors. Abusers will deny their actions and blaming you. Tell you that "You had that coming.""" Their attacks may begin verbally eventually moving into violence or patterns of domestic abuse.

They do this to show you who's boss and in control. Sometimes abuse comes in the form of acting possessive and will do everything they can to isolate you from family and friends. Not one of these things is acceptable. If this is happening, please get help.

Shaming/Humiliation- In any relationship it is a not-so-silent killer. It's one of the abuser's methods to manipulate you into feeling insecure.

They accomplish this by pointing out things they believe will make you feel horrible. Body shaming is a good example of this. I highly recommend Brene' Brown's books and TED Talks discussing this topic. She mentions actions like using your vulnerabilities against you, constantly comparing you to others, having no empathy for you, or using tone and body language to make you feel insignificant.

Withholding affection- Giving you the cold shoulder, acting aloof and dismissive are old tricks some manipulators use to get their way. Perhaps they were raised that way. Other reasons could stem from their emotional immaturity to deal with conflicts; it's their "go-to" behavior tactic as it's worked like a charm for them before. This falls under the controller persona. It may be a way to punish you for not getting what they want or you not doing what they asked you to do or something you may have said or done to them. They could have a mental illness or personality disorder. Be leery of such acts.

Telling someone you'll do something, which in your mind you "may do" unless a better opportunity comes up. Example: accepting two dates the same night and holding out for the better one in your mind.

Manipulation- Psychological, Emotional, Physical all come under this heading. Sadly, you may not be aware they are doing this as it's done covertly. They use guilt, insecurities, self-doubt, and make you responsible for their emotions. They are masterful at making you believe you want what they want. Knowing these warning signs early on will help you avoid these painful types of people.

Codependency- Oxford's dictionary states: "Excessive emotional or psychological reliance on a partner, typically one who requires support on account of an illness or addiction." "The tie that binds most of us together in this trap called codependency" Wikipedia puts it this way: "Codependency is a behavioral condition in a relationship where one person enables another person's addiction, poor mental health, immaturity, irresponsibility, or under-achievement."

Among the core characteristics of codependency is an excessive reliance on other people for approval and a sense of identity.

Watch for the following:

These people have extreme difficulty making any decisions in your relationship.

They have no clue as to identifying your feelings let alone knowing how to effectively communicate; often they value the approval of their friends over yours.

Making you feel bad for calling them out on their distasteful actions or behaviors.

Creating problems between two suitors that both want to be with you. You say things you know will rile them up while you sit back and watch the chaos unfolding. That is a sickness, my friend.

Not doing what you initially promised, making up excuses as to why you didn't. Then making the person you offered to help feel bad for asking.

Using something a person shared with you in confidence against them.

Repeating something someone told you in private and asked not to tell anyone and lying to that person saying you never told anyone.

Sharing personal things about your partner with their close friends or family members that would embarrass them.

"Ghosting" someone- Not returning phone calls, texts, or emails and saying you never received them.

Borrowing an item or money from your partner, never planning on giving or paying it back, and when they ask you for it, you tell them you thought it was a gift and how dare they ask you to give it back.

Playing one-upmanship during your relationship. Bad Juju!!

Going out of your way to make your partner jealous, again game over for me.

Saying things that you know will upset your partner.

ANGER ISSUES- Okay, this was my perpetual cross to bear. If you've read my previous book: *Taming the Anger Dragon, From Pissed off to Peaceful* then you know about my lifelong struggle with this issue.

I won't go into great detail here, but what I can say is I was one hell of an ANGRY MAN. Today, I consider myself a recovering anger-holic. It doesn't mean anger doesn't affect me. Oh, man, it still does, thankfully not to the degree it once had. My Anger Dragon had owned me. What I find ironic is that some of the things that just made me angry in others were my biggest hang-ups. Having someone else hurl their Anger Dragon at me was tantamount to a nuclear bomb exploding within me. 2500 years ago, Buddha said "You won't be punished for your anger; you will be punished by it." Great wisdom there. Anger issues left unresolved can create a living hell for both the giver and receiver and those caught in the crossfire. If you are currently in such a relationship or haven't resolved it within yourself, please seek professional help.

Loveless relationships- Sadly too many of us stay in unfulfilling relationships. Many are of convenience, all the while our soul feels like it's dying; a self-created life energy-zapping sentence of our own making. Yet, we choose to remain bound for a myriad of reasons, such as fear of being alone, financial loss, not wanting to disappoint our family or children, or feelings of unworthiness. The list goes on and on. The truth is when we settle for less than we deserve, most of us will suffer from feeling like something important in our life is missing, subsequently losing the joy of feeling fully alive. This sentiment will always be present in our subconscious. Many will sublimate these unrequited emotions. They knock them back with pills; work long hours, placate them with alcohol, or even extramarital affairs. All are detrimental to one's inner peace and well-being. No one said it would be easy to end. The question that begs to address is:

"What are your inner peace and personal happiness worth?"

Words to the wise; to thine own self be true. Go for happy.

In closing, many of the things mentioned could all go under the header called toxic relationships. When we give ourselves the love we are seeking, we come to the relationship table as an equal, not willing to settle for mediocrity. We dare to set boundaries. If we've recently ended a toxic relationship, we give ourselves time to heal. Know in your heart of hearts, any abuse thrown at you was NOT your responsibility.

You did NOT deserve it.

You will not allow those patterns of behavior to exist in your next one.

When we play these mind games, there are no winners.

Have you recognized any of those dysfunctional characteristics in relationships?

How have you detoxified?

Thomas E. Ziemann

If you remain in that type of relationship or keep attracting toxic dynamics in subsequent unions, ask yourself how you can disentangle from them.

CHAPTER 27:

I AM WOMAN, HEAR ME ROAR

"I raise up my voice, not so that I can shout, but so that those without a voice can be heard. We cannot all succeed when half of us are held back."
~Malala Yousafzai

Gender stereotypes are degrading and can hurt a woman's self-confidence. These falsehoods and ill-conceived notions belong in history's trash bin.

I added a few that sprung to mind.

Powerful women are bitches.- I find it ironic that a man is referred to as a strong leader when he acts like an ass to his subordinates. However if a woman takes charge, she's bitchy. Insecure men continue this fabrication.

Single women are lonely.- As discussed in the previous chapter on singlehood this is patently false. Being alone is not the same as being lonely.

Women are hyper-emotional.- My experience is that women operate more from their emotions, but it isn't always excessive expression. Hormonal changes may intensify emotions.

Women are overly sensitive.- This goes both ways, depends on the person. Sensitivity to the feelings of others enhances relationship intimacy.

Girls are not good at sports.- Virtually any skill can be developed. Today's women have gone into the boxing ring; have pitched no-hitters, coach in the NFL, compete in NASCAR, and the Daytona 500 and win Olympic Gold medals.

Masculine women are all lesbians.- Misogynists use this misconception and generality to this day. There are some women who love other women who are masculine presenting and some feminine appearing.

Women are only concerned about physical appearance. Perhaps vapid women fall into this category. Its true women tend to be more attentive to the way they look to others than men; however, that's only one small aspect of the whole person.

Blonds are less intelligent than other women.- Another fabrication. Women can have any hair color they desire; the dye doesn't make them stupid. Moreover my ex-wife Shannon was known as a towhead as she was called by her siblings. They were also dirty blonds. She is perhaps one of the wisest people I've ever met. She probably boasts an IQ of over 150.

She just loved kicking my ass at Jeopardy and Trivial Pursuit. She spanked me yearly, game after game. Never let me win nor forget who bested me. Never once did I win. It gave me great delight when my buddy Alan challenged her to play Trivial Pursuit and he beat her. LOVED THAT.

Women who have many cats will never get a man.- What a load. My wife is a total babe. We both had five cats each when we moved in together after our marriage. All 10 cats got along surprisingly well.

All librarians are women, they are old, wear glasses, and have a perpetual frown on their face. Most are spinsters.- Got news for ya, my oldest daughter Caitlin graduated from Queens College with her master's in library sciences; a difficult degree to obtain. She is incredibly bright. While she does wear stylin' glasses, she's got a wonderful man in her life. So much for this generality.

Only an anorexic woman can become a runway model. Another weak generality. Women of all sizes and shapes strut their stuff on stage and pose for magazine covers.

A woman's place is in the house.- I agree......and the Senate. The 2018 national election was incredibly refreshing; to see all the women who have entered the political field and won the greatest number of seats in congress and political offices than ever in the history of the US.

Here's a list of current Female Worldwide leaders from TIME Magazine all reportedly piloting their countries successfully, thus debunking the myth that women are too emotional to lead.

Helle Thorning-Schmidt, Prime Minister of Denmark

Yingluck Shinawatra, Prime Minister of Thailand

Angela Merkel, Chancellor of Germany

Cristina Fernández de Kirchner, President of Argentina

Dilma Rousseff, President of Brazil

Julia Gillard, Prime Minister of Australia

Ellen Johnson Sirleaf, President of Liberia

Sheik Hasina Wajed, Prime Minister of Bangladesh

Johanna Sigurdardottir, Prime Minister of Iceland

Laura Chinchilla, President of Costa Rica

Tarja Halonen, President of Finland

Dalia Grybauskaite, President of Lithuania

Kamla Persad-Bissessar, Prime Minister of Trinidad and Tobago

Jacinda Kate Laurell Ardern, Prime Minister of New Zealand

A woman should remain barefoot and pregnant.- WTF? Only barefoot by choice as she walks on fresh green grass and digs her toes in the sand. The decision to become pregnant is hers, in collaboration with her partner if they both desire parenting.

Women are bad drivers.- HELLO, bad drivers come from both sides of the road.

After a brief discussion on gender roles, Michelle and I went back to sipping our beers. The early evening sun was keeping it comfy on the deck. I asked her some questions about her own beliefs about relationships which seem apropos to include here.

She sat with silent lucidity for a few moments and shared a few ideas (in no particular order.)

She wanted me to remind people to simply enjoy the journey of dating. Learn to make friends along the way. It's okay if it doesn't work out romantically.

If you share that truth with your soon to be former boyfriend and he can't accept just being platonic pals he wasn't the one. What does matter is how you developed personally.

Michelle then mentioned the most important lesson she had gleaned during her dating days and LTRs was learning to set boundaries. Before meeting me, she finally had mastered the ability of not losing herself to simply please her man. In her past relationships, when she lost herself, she lost at the end, self-respect and dignity that is.

Michelle's single time allowed her the freedom to be her own boss. With time, she learned to enjoy her own company. She filled her weekends with volunteering at a local animal shelter where we met. She moved into a condo and created her magical sanctuary, filling it with things she loved. And cats, many cats, which in no way make her that stereotypical old cat lady. My buddies joke with me saying I am the old cat lady, by the way.

She spent time honing her artistic side as well, writing blogs, baking, creating artwork, painting, and more. It filled her soul with peace as she had no experience prior. For the first time in her adult life she was okay with not needing to be with a man. Sure, she admitted sometimes she was lonely; however those longing feelings didn't last long. She sublimated her wanting by reading spiritual and uplifting books. One that had a profound lasting effect on her life was written by Swami Chetanananda called *Open Heart, Open Mind*, which is a classic book about spiritual awakening.

The *5 Love Languages* as well as books by Eckhart Tolle, Iyanla Vanzant and Stephanie Dowrick helped round out her emotional understanding and needs.

Late in life, Michelle figured out how to love herself which inexorably changed her life. Forgiveness on many levels allowed this to happen. Had neither of us taken the time to work on ourselves, we never would have been ready nor met each other.

What myths have you believed about women?

What were the sources of that misinformation?

Have you shaken off those fabrications?

CHAPTER 69:

MAKING LOVE OR HAVING SEX, THE CHOICES ARE ENDLESS

"Good sex is like good bridge.
If you don't have a good partner,
you'd better have a good hand."
~ Mae West

Hot, Steamy, Erotic, Intimate, Animalistic, Fleshy, Alluring, Torrid, Rhythmic, Mind-Blowing, Body Shaking, Explosive, Electrifying, and Orgasmic... a cacophony of intense emotions like no other ravages my once rational mind. Fueled by childlike excitement; suspenseful anticipation, sultry angst-filled exhilaration extenuated with expectation all playing a fiery, lustful symphony in concert that erupts deep within my body; similar to the addict's first hit. Likened to a sumptuous eleven-course gastronomic feast, driven with passion, spark-like sensations instantaneously surge. Dopamine is being released in the nucleus accumbens of my brain's pleasure center. Hot breath deepens; pulsating hot blood circulates like wildfire through my enlarged veins, pupils dilate overcome with wanton desire. Heart ventricles open wider to accommodate the additional oxygen required for copulation, intensified, intoxicating carnal desires all setting the stage for explosive, climactic sweat-filled finale draining every living cell in my flushed body!

OK! You've decided to take the plunge and moved your relationship to the physical aspect; hopefully, this time you have gotten to know each other first to make it even more special. Great advice that I wish I had followed in my earlier relationships.

More perhaps has been written about sex than about love. It's been fought over, killed for, and paid for. There are thousands of different kinds of sex; some that heal, some that fulfill, some that leave one desiring more. Some sex is funny, and some is fun. Fulfilling sex simultaneously gives energy that can be claimed upon waking up. Great sex opens or creates pathways, which allow energy to travel throughout the participant's body. It's drug-releasing endorphins and serotonin.

Author and speaker Deepak Chopra said "Sex is always about emotions. Good sex is about free emotions; bad sex is about blocked emotions."

For most people, sex is pleasurable, a necessary part of their relationship. Sexual compatibility and communication they believe is vitally important for long term love which supports their lasting relationship; it helps maintain it.

I like the concept of Tantric sex; an ancient Hindu practice that has been going for well over 5,000 years. Tantric means 'the weaving and expansion of energy'. It's a slow form of sex that's said to increase intimacy and create a mind-body connection that can lead to powerful orgasms. When you orgasm, there's a flood of oxytocin and vasopressin. Those neurochemicals are linked with the attachment system in the brain.

My best friend and wife Michelle mentioned she passionately believes that for her and many women sex takes place in the mind well before she hops into bed. She refers this to as mental foreplay, combining intelligence and stimulation.

Canadian scientists from McGill University have discovered that intellectual stimulation is more linked to women's sexual arousal than men's.

Studies recorded that PET scans show that during sex, the parts of the female brain responsible for processing fear, anxiety, and emotion start to relax more and more, reaching a peak at orgasm, when the female brain's anxiety and emotion are effectively closed down.

Our sex drive is largely orchestrated by testosterone in both men and women, but romantic love is orchestrated by the dopamine system. Sexual activity comes complete with a complicated mix of emotions; expectations, hopes, fears, and taboos that shape our sexual lives.

I read somewhere that sexual compatibility has been defined as; to the extent in which a couple perceives they share sexual beliefs; preferences, expectations, desires, values, and needs and sex drive will more or less match the other. It's the degree couples are on the same page in the boudoir. Don't be alarmed if it doesn't happen right away; things may take time to ripen, on the other hand married couples often divorce over sexual incompatibility as discussed in an earlier chapter.

Different levels of libido have been cited as a common complaint. She wants sex daily, he only a couple of times a week. He prefers oral, but she is turned off by having to perform it and so on.

Jim Heaphy studied Human Sexuality at the City College of San Francisco and said, "In my opinion, that term would describe the relationship between a couple that finds it extremely easy to come to an agreement about various aspects of their mutual sexual activity. For example, this may include frequency of sexual encounters, variety of positions and sex acts, length of time of the sexual encounters, issues of inhibition and modesty, and frequency of orgasm for both partners. Cheerful willingness to compromise is an important aspect of sexual compatibility."

There are several quizzes you can find online which you can take with your partner to delve even deeper as to both of your preferences, etc. One way to tell if you are sexually compatible is if you both your bodies and mind align during intercourse.

This brings us to Sexual Communication; developing the type of relationship where both partners can share their deepest desires without feeling shame, guilt, anxiety, or being judged afterward. One where they can discuss openly and freely what turns them on, how they "Like" it, and what they need to reach orgasm without blushing or feeling uncomfortable. "Pinch here, poke that, rub here" can be shared without ridicule. Having this type of communication is like an insurance policy for your future together. Being able to share this type of openness will often open up other areas thereby allowing and promoting deeper communication in your lives. It's my fervent belief that there ought not to be no subjects that a couple can't at least discuss.

Walter Last put it this way: "Sexuality is closely related to spirituality in several ways. In its negative aspects of lust, sexual excess, degradation, and rape, it appears as the antithesis of spirituality, and in this light it has been seen in the Christian tradition. However, in its positive aspects, our sexuality can open our heart to love, and enable us to have experienced similar to meditative states and mystical bliss during or instead of an orgasm and its afterglow."

The best quote I have ever read on sex comes from Alexandra Katehakis in her book, *Erotic Intelligence*: "Spiritualizing sex is a movement of energy-feeling and emotion—that rises within you and moves into your sexual physicality as an alive, tender, erotic, or passionate expression. Your bodies move without inhibition so all the energy can flow out of you and between the two of you. You allow spiritual energy to express its dance through you. Sexuality can be a profound demonstration of your love, and especially your freedom, to express and bond. Spiritual sex, then, combines how you express your love with the intentions or blessings you bring to your partnership."

In closing, it is important to remember that choosing the right partner is critical!

It can help you avoid many issues that arise as the relationship moves on from the honeymoon phase to the long-term stage. Figuring out what works to keep yours fresh and alive is your ticket to paradise.

Do you live orgasmically in and out of the bedroom?

Are you aware of your needs and desires?

Can you share them with a partner, openly and without embarrassment?

CHAPTER 28:

DEATH, DEARLY DEPARTED AND LOST RELATIONSHIPS, MAY THEY REST IN PEACE

"Death ends a life, not a relationship."
~ Mitch Albom

As we come near to the close of my part of the book, I thought it befitting to end by focusing on a subject most of us don't welcome discussions about. The truth is that all things perish. It's the natural cycle of life. Death's ravenous maw spares no one. A permanent cessation of all vital functions, a test nobody fails. Everyone you know will someday die or leave you or you will die or leave them. No one in history has ever cheated it. An old Italian proverb states, "After the game, the king and the pawn go into the same box." Many people fear it; perhaps not the dying part, but simply having to face the unknown. However, since it must come to pass, why not embrace it?

The sooner we come to terms with our own eventual leave taking, the more peace we can experience.

I love Eckhart Tolle's quote: "Death is a stripping away of all that is not you. The secret of life is to "die before you die and find that there is no death." Once I came to terms with my own mortality, it felt as though a large boulder had been lifted off me. It taught me to live in the moment, more mindfully as the Buddha taught.

Death reminds us not to rush past the things we'll wish we had more of at the very end of life. Endeavor not to be the person on his or her deathbed lamenting the things they wish they'd done or tried. Sadly, what we put off are often the things that prove to be our greatest satisfaction in life. Here's something else to consider; we are all dying a little each day. Our entire physical body is changed every seven years, our skin cells about every 30 days, stomach lining about every 45 days. We literally are not the same person we were when we went to sleep the night before. Therefore, it's preferable to be more concerned with what we keep in our hearts, mind, and spirit while traveling through life. That stated, I am of the opinion that one's soul cannot be destroyed. The brave may not live forever but the cowardly never live at all. Since it's useless to worry about the inevitable, it's absolutely freeing and liberating to accept death and be at peace with one's own life concluding.

In this way, we all can meet it with dignity, daring, and joy, as well as adding value and purpose to our lives right now.

"The tragedy of life is not death, it's what we let die inside ourselves when we are alive." ~Norman Cousins

So where am I going with this, you may be questioning? I feel there are similarities in deaths we experience, whether it is a friend, family member, beloved pet, to the death of a relationship. Sometimes it's both. Truth for me is all relationships have eternal life. They continue in our memories. Sometimes without our control, they sneak out of our eyes down our cheeks. How we frame our memories of them has much to do with how they affect us. While we cannot change the past, we can change our perception of it.

Sagely advice is to make peace with your past. Focus on the beauty of a person and their qualities you loved. The precious moments you shared, the good times. The difficult times hold equal wisdom in that they all offered lessons for you. Of course there may be relationships that ended poorly and were filled with pain. You have suffered

297

enough already. Time to forgive both yourself and the other. Not because they deserve it. Do it for the inner peace you will experience by doing so. Holding anger, hatred, and disdain towards them only hurts you.

Buddha said two things that resonate strongly with me here.

1st- "Holding on to anger is like grasping a hot coal with the intent of throwing it at someone else; you are the one who gets burned."

2nd-"Holding on to anger is like drinking poison and hoping the other dies."

Great wisdom indeed. August Wilson wrote, "Your willingness to wrestle with your demons will cause your angels to sing."

Forgiveness is a magical elixir. It's one of the only things I know of without any bad side effects. Whether they care or if they are even alive today matters not. What does matter is how it will make you feel. Forgiveness doesn't mean forgetting the past. It's coming to terms with it. Accepting what happen and allowing yourself to move beyond what happened. By doing so, you release a heavy burden.

Pain is a marvelous master teacher. If we heed its lessons, we usually only have to deal with them a single time. Bryant H. McGill made a beautiful observation. He said, "There is no love without forgiveness, and there is no forgiveness without love." Forgiveness elevates the spirit while transforming relationships.

Love is the secret, The Alpha, and the Omega. It is the tool to release those old hurts. Love is the lubricant that oils the wheels of forgiveness.

Death is something I am keenly familiar with all too well. To help assuage my pain and begin the grieving cycle, I would post blogs on Facebook. I found it to be a way to accelerate the process and also shorten its duration

Losing both my parents and four cherished cats in such short succession has certainly given me much to ponder, process, and work through. Writing these posts has helped me diminish the pain and hopefully add another perspective for those who too are suffering. One never knows who they may touch by sharing their pain and deepest feelings.

A follower on my page reminded me that "It is not about never feeling pain again. It is about feeling it fully and finding the beauty in our suffering." Many thanks for all of the heartfelt outpouring of your kindness. It's truly meaningful. It's times like this, one reaps the benefits of their friendship garden they have cultivated. Our wonderful caring friends, close and afar are the ones that help lessen the burden of great loss and sorrow. It's focusing on things that I am profoundly grateful for that's helping heal and close these painfully deep emotional wounds.

That said, I wanted to share a few points on grieving. Anyone can write about it, however, when one experiences it firsthand, it adds clarity and thoughts which may help others during tumultuous times. Everyone you know is most likely fighting some kind of personal battle or issue whether they share it openly or not.

Thoughts on Grieving

1- Everyone must come to terms with their tribulations in their own way and time. What may be a few days for some, may take other people years to process. I have a dear Facebook friend who said she still cries daily even though her father died nine months ago. I believe this is good since it is helping her to heal and cleanse her heart.

2- If one doesn't allow themselves to grieve, it most likely will fester thereby creating future problems in other areas of their lives. Of course dealing with grief's sting head-on will be painful, once dealt with allows healing to commence.

3- During the grieving process, figure out what you need to alleviate your suffering. It might be getting online help as I have chosen to do. Sharing my pain and receiving a myriad of uplifting wishes from family, friends, and confidants provided comfort. One might need time alone, quiet time to ponder and organize their thoughts. Perhaps prayer or meditation will be of value, finding solace in their place of worship, church, synagogue, or temple. Seeking the services of an experienced therapist has been shown to have a plethora of long term, lasting benefits. Spending quality, undisturbed time with friends or family may be your ticket. Acclaimed MD Andrew Weil talks about the benefits of herbal remedies, such as Holy Basil, St John's Wort and SamE. He also suggests adding flowers and plants for one's home and workspace. Sharing meals can be wonderful. Walks along the beach, mountains, desert, forest, or even a stroll through a local park might be your thing. You might consider writing a letter to the person and express everything you didn't get to share with them while they were alive.

Perhaps even having a little ceremony and burying or burning the note with loving prayers and thoughts could help with a sense of closure. The key is doing something that is meaningful to you. Only you will know what works. Be certain not to neglect your cherished pets during this time, they may not know what happened, only that something is wrong. Let them help heal you with their unconditional love that only a pet can provide.

4- Stay busy. Get out of your house. Sublimate your feelings with good works; perhaps volunteering at your local humane shelter. Start those nagging projects you have been meaning to do, not only will it help take your mind off your pain but will accomplish something you decided you needed to do. In this way, you will have something to show for your efforts. Be certain to reward yourself after doing so, whatever floats your boat, whether it is a nurturing massage, a sumptuous dinner, that bottle of wine/champagne you've always wanted to sample but couldn't justify the expense. Maybe a trip to the coast. Whatever you believe will help you feel better just as long as it's not self-destructive.

5- Stop the negative self-talk on what you did or didn't do. There's no good in rumination on the past that you can't change. I'm guessing you did the absolute best you could within the limits of your awareness at the time.

6- Allowing the healing power of forgiveness to work its magic. Whether it be forgiving the actions of another or ourselves. We forgive not because the other deserves it, we do it to give ourselves inner peace.

7- A major tenet in Buddhism is attachments and their relationship to suffering. Figuring out how to release your own will provide a lifetime of benefits.

8- Remember the caring people who were there for you during your painful time and extend that grace to others. Since you've been there, you can be the light. At the same time, you will benefit emotionally and spiritually from consoling another. Just allowing the other to talk will be enough.

9- Allow yourself to fully accept your situation, realizing that time generally heals all. Fully loving and accepting yourself as you are, remember that you are enough. Additionally, appreciate the blessing of the relationship you once had. Celebrate the fond memories which added meaning to your life.

10- Being Present and Mindful, as the greatest teachers past and present remind us to "be here now." Ram Dass, Eckhart Tolle, Gandhi, and Buddha made this a huge part of their lessons to alleviate suffering. By doing so we appreciate what's happening and enjoy and live more fully.

People often ask why I sculpt pumpkins and watermelons. The reason is that they do not last. They must be enjoyed in the present which can add fond memories for the recipient. The same is true for our relationships. No one knows how long they have. Far better to show gratitude for the gift of friendships we experience.

In closing this chapter, my ardent desire for you the reader is that the messages inside this book will serve as a redemptive reminder, that creating your dream relationship is indeed possible. It must be created from within you. By you becoming the person you have sought all these years, you attract them. Use the suggestions you found helpful herein and make them work in your favor.

Nowhere in this book did it say it would be a piece of cake, far from it. It will take work on your part; fortitude, and continuous effort to create and cultivate your relationship of a lifetime. It will require emotional gardening and tender daily care to maintain it and keep your relationship healthy, growing, and strong.

It may not be easy; however, I promise you that the rewards you receive will be incredible.

I love you all.

What are the goodbyes you have said throughout your life?

Do you still carry those people in your heart?

If the relationship ended badly, are you making peace with the loss?

CHAPTER 29:

SUGGESTIONS TO ENHANCE YOUR INNER PEACE

"The psychotic drowns in the same waters in which the mystic swims with delight."
~ Joseph Campbell

The book is nearing the end. I thought it fitting to make the last chapter uplifting. One that would add perspective, solace, and pick us up when we were feeling down. Powerful ideas designed to ignite one's soul, adding inspiration, hope, and wisdom.

I am a huge fan of Malcolm Gladwell. I love his savvy writing style; how he masterfully interweaves some of the earlier parts of his narrative throughout his book, so much so that I am taking a page out of his writing playbook. A few of the thoughts added into this chapter have been previously mentioned. Repetition is the mother of skill. It allows one to ponder and take in ideas. If they make sense to us, we can add them to our ways of thinking.

Today, millions of people are suffering worldwide. Global pandemic, war-torn countries creating a refugee problem greater than one could imagine, with accompanying starvation. I feel their pain daily. Our planet is taking a beating as well. Coral reefs are slowly dying, glaciers melting. Once bountiful rain forests are being devastated at unconscionably accelerated rates. Animals are rapidly nearing extinction. It breaks my heart. We hear about these heart-wrenching things in the news daily. The media loves reporting pain as it sells newspapers and gets ratings. Much like a car crash, one's morbid curiosity gets the better of them and they have to look.

That said, some of this chapter was borrowed from my previous books; *The Department of Zenitation: A laymen's guide to making spirituality work in real life* and *Taming the Anger Dragon: From Pissed off the Peaceful.*

I felt by combining them they added deeper meaning and understanding to some of the concepts suggested. It made the book feel whole; greater than the sum of its parts and added hope.

Think of the following suggestions like the spiritual grease that helps lubricate your inner emotional machine. Many of the ideas were gathered from some of the greatest inspiration I have ever read and loved.

New Beginnings

The New Year is a time to consider the promise of new beginnings; prosperity, and greater fulfillment in one's life.

I speak not only of material wealth but of Harmonious Relationships, Spiritual Growth, Emotional Maturity, and Inner Peace. Like the New Year, the Phoenix represents one's rebirth, the letting go of the past and embracing a brand-new outlook on life. A good analogy is that of the snake shedding its skin, and it can be likened to throwing off old habits, attitudes, relationships, and other things that no longer serve our greater nature.

Everyone you know has been hurt. Forgiveness is a magic elixir that will give you freedom from suffering. Only the strong can fully do this. This doesn't mean those that hurt you remain part of your life. Acknowledge your pain. Find out its lesson and let it go. While it's not easy, it is necessary, if you are to be free. Good things will come your way simply by believing you are worthy of such.

Letting People Go

It can be hard to let people go from our lives or be let go of ourselves. Time usually proves it was prudent for having done so. That said, it still doesn't make it easy.

I've done this when I didn't feel people were there for me or supported me. Life is too short. I forgive them. Some have come back into my life, others haven't, and it's all worked out. One doesn't have to be a prick or be mean about it either. Time has a miraculous way of healing if we allow it. If they don't nourish my soul, I let them go. Something that I have found helpful is remembering that I had a full, rich life before someone came into it and will have a full, rich life once we have moved on.

Another is knowing that although I never close anyone out of my heart, I choose to close the door and wish them well and even love them from a safe distance. Love is never wasted. Demonstrating congruence is something that takes practice, courage, and maturity to do. You gain much by continuing down this path of self-love.

Self-Care

One cannot pour from an empty pitcher; we must take care of ourselves first. Satisfying one's own needs is critical, not selfish. Have you noticed when flying what every airline mandates before taking off, the flight attendants are required by law to give the passengers a safety briefing. They always say that in the case of a loss in cabin pressure to put your mask on first before attempting to put one on another. Lots of wisdom there. And there's nothing selfish about it. Author, educator, and activist, Parker J. Palmer nicely sums this up perfectly:

"Self-care is never a selfish act – it is simply good stewardship of the only gift I have, the gift I was put on earth to offer others. Anytime we can listen to true self and give the care it requires, we do it not only for ourselves but for the many others whose lives we touch".

Go Where You Are Celebrated Rather Than Merely Tolerated

Tis' my belief that everyone/everything is connected, some are immediately recognized and felt. Energies gravitate towards each other and seek similar vibrations. These special connections are part of your spiritual tribe that transcends time and space. You found each other for a reason. It is my deep conviction that Universal Mind (a.k.a. Source) wastes no time with mere coincidence.

The trick is figuring out why, and not letting these important connections slip away. So often we hunger for others to love us, the truth is simply by loving and accepting ourselves we fully open the Floodgates of Universal Love.

This is not some New Age idea. It is real and has been disseminated by the earliest wise ones for eons. I love this quote: "Connection doesn't care about the laws of the land; your soul will be pulled to the place it belongs." (Author Unknown).

No More People Pleasing

People-pleasing has been a longtime issue for me. In the past, when I would head out to town to catch a show or to a party, I would hope people would like me. As time went on, I gave myself the deep love I was searching for.

Now when I am invited to a party, I'm hoping I will find someone who's interesting to talk to. I don't care if they like me. I'm not for everyone. I'm not saying this in an egotistical way. Just a fact I've come to accept. Our expectation of ourselves is the answer. No one else's, period. There comes a time when we just tell people NO. We can't. We don't have to be mean about it, just frank. People may not like it, but they will respect us more for being upfront than tellin' them we will do something which we never wanted to do in the first place and may let them down by not doing what we offered. Stay true to thyself. You'll be happier, I promise.

Become Your Own Best Friend: It Begins Within

Are you seeking an incredible, loving relationship with someone? Perhaps you haven't met them yet or the initial spark seems to have dwindled in your current relationship. It's my fervent belief that real love for others always "Begins from Within" by becoming your own best friend. Unless you accept yourself completely, fully, and unconditionally it's unlikely you will attract, develop, or enjoy the magnificent fruits of what a fulfilling relationship can bestow. I'm not speaking of narcissism here, simply openly and honestly accepting yourself wholly, your gifts, shortcomings, and those pesky demons you haven't yet dealt with. Your self-talk has dramatic, impactful effects on every aspect of your life. Lighten up on yourself; you'll gain a happier, more satisfying daily existence. Take time today to give yourself the love you've been seeking and watch the magic unfold.

Set an Intention for Everyday

A daily intention I read from a dear friend that I love goes like this: "Have extraordinary experiences and connect with amazing people." She says this each morning before she gets out of bed and it has transformed her life. As I plot my daily plan I am reminded of the wonderful quote from child

development researcher and founder and director of
the advocacy and consulting group, Little
Hearts/Gentle Parenting Resources, L. R. Knost: "Life
is amazing. And then it's awful. And then it's amazing
again. And in between the amazing and the awful, it's
ordinary and mundane and routine. Breathe in the
amazing, hold on through the awful, and relax and
exhale during the ordinary. That's just living
heartbreaking, soul-healing, amazing, awful, ordinary
life. It's breathtakingly beautiful."

Understanding and Using the Law of Attraction

Recently there have been a multitude of books and
movies discussing this universal principle. It's most
basic understanding can be answered with the
following question: Why do positive expectations have
a much better chance of becoming reality? It's been
proposed for thousands of years by some of the wisest
sages. Our intentions are powerful! They can help
manifest profound results. They create vibrations in the
Planck scale level, described by and named after
theoretical physicist, Max Planck. This theory has been
described for many years in Quantum Mechanics and
garnered Planck the Nobel Prize in Physics in 1918.
These ripples transcend time and space. I refer to this
as "Universal Vibrational Response." The Universe
doesn't care what vibrations one chooses. It doesn't

judge…it simply returns. Call it what you like. Is this foolproof?

While nothing in life is ever guaranteed, a healthy mix of unbound enthusiasm, tempered with realistic expectations, favors the hopeful and increases one's chances exponentially. Keep in mind that effort and work need to accompany one's positive expectations. While one's intentions are especially important, without love and action they rarely manifest into anything worthwhile.

As mentioned previously, the movie *The Secret* shared the message of intention to a wide audience. But good intentions alone will not be enough. It's the doing part that creates the magic. Note: The Law of Attraction is a double-edged sword. When we focus on negative thinking, act in hateful ways, it believes that is what we are looking for and sends the things we fear. In my mind, it's not a judging thing, in other words it doesn't care what you hold in your mind. You think about it enough and WHAMMO, you begin to draw that to you. Therefore be incredibly mindful of what you want, don't want, fear, hate, and so on.

To reiterate, I believe Rhonda Byrnes' follow-up to *The Secret*, called *The Power* shared this message in a far deeper context and didn't mainly focus on material wealth. Having been dealt some devastating emotional blows in my life, it's become painfully obvious that change happens. I'm no quitter. While change can be difficult to embrace, it's necessary.

My main hourly goal is to want more than anything else to feel good at this very moment. Ask yourself: "How would it feel now, this very second?" What would help you? What specifically would be different? It's been said that by what circumstance, we grow.

Murky thoughts obtain lackluster results at best. When it comes to using Universal Vibrational Response, you must focus on EXACTLY what will help you. Act as if it already exists in your mind. Don't concern yourself with how it will manifest.

Just believing that you are worthy is enough. Again, this is not some pie in the sky "woo woo" advice, it's been taught by the earliest sages and truth seekers.

The bottom line is that intentions plus action help to create your destiny.

Know Thyself

If you take away just one point from this entire book, this is it: Your inner peace will be greatly enhanced by knowing who you are, and why you think and believe the way you do. Only you can answer this question. Knowing your anger and joy triggers add to one's self-knowledge and are critical for making lasting, meaningful changes. I love the adage that simply states:

"Your perception of me is a direct reflection of you. My reaction to you is an inner awareness of me."

As Shakespeare wrote, "To thine own self be true," voiced by Polonius in Hamlet. Only you can determine what path/person is best suited for you. Those chosen for us rarely bring long term self-satisfaction. Knowing who you are, what makes you happy, and knowing SPECIFICALLY what you are looking for adds magic to any endeavor or relationship. Only you can answer what will truly fulfill your spiritual, physical, and emotional needs.

Never Apologize for Who You Are

An amazing transformation happens to us when we finally accept and come to terms with who we truly are. No more putting up walls of defense, no more worrying about what people think. No more burdens of keeping up false personas or pretenses. You may be pleasantly surprised by the sheer number of people who love you for who you truly are.

As musician, coach, and inspirational speaker Jason Hairston eloquently stated: "Being considered crazy by those who are still the victims of cultural conditioning is a compliment."

Don't Be for Everyone

I mentioned a few years ago, I was throwing a few icy cold ones back with one of my best mates Marc. I had been saving one of our favorite, top-shelf 100% silver agave tequilas "El Tesoro". We were laughing and feeling no pain. I could tell that Marc wanted to tell me something that seemed important. He said he didn't want to hurt my feelings. Now I had to know what the hell he was talking about. I kept needling him until he finally spilled. He looked right at me and said. "Tom…. you're not for everybody……but you are for me." I was taken totally off guard and wasn't sure that I liked the sound of that. I smiled and said "You betcha!" I pondered what he said for several days and when the truth finally sunk in, I was elated and knew he was correct. It taught me a life-changing, valuable lesson that being true to thyself is far more important than trying to please everyone. I wear that commendation with pride these days.

Invest in Those Who Invest in You

From that day I realized Marc's meaning. I made it a practice to invest heavily in my tribe. This didn't mean I suddenly blew off my other acquaintances, but it meant I focused my deepest attention and love on those who celebrated our friendship as opposed to those who merely tolerated me. Rest assured its far better planting the seeds of love in a fertile, welcoming garden as opposed to trying to break ground on a hard-pan lifeless field of aloofness.

Question Everything

Our perspective determines how we experience anything. As I mentioned in my first book, *The Department of Zenitation*, think of truth as a multi-faceted gemstone. It glimmers in many directions, all the light coming from the same beautiful stone. Ancient societies have proclaimed the three stages of truth as 1- ridicule 2 - violent opposition and 3- acceptance. Inner peace, balance, and happiness start with and are reinforced by the truth. Fundamental truths are those that transcend cultures and different belief systems. The truth can set you free, but can you handle it? Most of us believe that what we feel is the truth. Much of the time, it is only a vague and partial reality.

The truth is one, but the paths are many. What's true for one may not be true for another. Your truth and **the** truth are two separate things. The truth is relative, depending on where one stands. Any lasting, meaningful relationship must be built upon it. Don't tell half-truths and expect trust when the full truth comes out, as it usually does in the long run, half-truths are no better than lies. There is often a kernel of truth interwoven with every misconception.

Contents are always more important than packaging. Choose to be led by specific evidence rather than your personal beliefs.

Use Gratitude as Your Helmsman

Gratitude heals and rewards both the giver and receiver. Living the "Attitude of Gratitude" keeps the door open to abundance and prosperity. It's not happiness that brings us gratitude, it's gratitude that brings us happiness. If you make the conscious decision to become happier and more grateful, this motivation will play a significant role in manifesting incredible things. I've witnessed firsthand the beauty when someone goes out of their way to make life beautiful for others. Make this a part of your daily practice and watch the magic that unfolds! The giver often receives an even greater benefit by having done so. I used to get really depressed and super disappointed when I thought that people would do as I would have done for them, and this was an unrealistic expectation on my part.

I overcame my misplaced anger by remembering that not everyone has the same mindset which I carry. This doesn't make them bad people. We are simply different people. I honestly believe that gratitude and compassion are cut from the same cloth. They operate within the same field of energy at the quantum level, creating joy in both the giver and receiver. A most compassionate act is doing something with a grateful heart that the receiver can never repay you for. One daily practice I do is coming up with 20 things on the spot when I can't sleep, or I am feeling frustrated. I've also created a gratitude jar which I put notes of things that made me happy during that day. I save them up till the end of the year. On New Year's Eve I pop a nice bottle of Champagne and relive all those wonderful, happy memories.

A gratitude journal might be more your cup of tea. They both work well. Try it for yourself.

Discover Your Life's Purpose

When I hit the big 5-0 I discovered something that changed my daily life. I finally figured out exactly what my Life Purpose was. It has made me feel more whole. It's given me a reason to give more of myself daily. Only you can answer these burning questions: Why are you here? What will be your legacy? What will you be remembered for? If you can clearly define your Life Purpose in 15 words or less, congratulations: you're in the top 5% of the entire world. I commend you. My Life Purpose is helping others to define theirs. I work toward it daily, have since figured it out. Don't worry if you're not sure what yours is. It gives you something to ponder and discover. Don't be concerned if it changes. Age and life changes can give one a different perspective and what direction we have moved into.

This one insight is perhaps the greatest gift you could ever give yourself. It gives meaning to your daily existence. Without knowing exactly what your life's calling is, it's unlikely you will be truly spiritually fulfilled, as a result, you will live half of what you could have accomplished. Hopefully, this is taken as an inspiring message of self-fulfillment and personal growth.

Anyone regardless of gender, race, creed, background or upbringing can do this. To see yourself already having accomplished your goals is powerful medicine. There's incredible inner power in defining your purpose. This one simple act can positively effect and act as a catapult creating profound changes in your life forever! Affirming yours will open many doors that you may not even have been aware of. Don't ignore the opportunities being presented to you. Pay attention, look for them. Most importantly act on them and trust your gut feelings. I speak from experience.

Many serendipitous things happened to me once I finally started my first book *The Department of Zenitation* in earnest. It took me 32 years to bring it to fruition. I never quit. The reviews it has garnered on Amazon etc. tell me it's touched readers' lives in a positive way. Don't worry that your dreams are too large. Once you figure out why you're here, leave it to a force greater than yourself.

Attachments

Attachments are a central part of Buddhism's teachings – and the suffering they can bring. Attachments can range from addictions to overeating, excessive spending, gambling problems, sex compulsions, drugs, excessive alcohol, detrimental relationships, and much more.

The way our brains are wired is that it takes an even greater amount of whatever one desires to achieve a perceived greater satisfaction state. The aftermath of a 'high' is generally associated with incredible lows. One doesn't need to become a Buddhist to gain the benefits from its inherent wisdom. Simply recognizing what your attachments are, then deciding whether you are ready to let them go will bring greater self-awareness of what controls you. Moderation is the key. Self-Love is a critical part of any meaningful, lasting change.

Daily Random Acts of Kindness

Kindness is the willingness to give of oneself to others and performing such acts without any expectation afterward creates deep lasting self-satisfaction; especially to people (or animals) who can never repay you. When I'm feeling low, I reach out and touch people. It's not hard to give a kind word or a tender smile. How one treats people they don't have to be nice to define them. As Mark Twain once said: "Kindness is the language which the deaf can hear and the blind can see." While the sheer act of intention may add a nice warm and fleeting, fuzzy feeling, the reward is how these simple acts make you feel after having performed them.

Proactive Listening

I've made a conscientious daily commitment to becoming a better communicator. This begins with listening. One way to directly measure someone's intelligence and emotional maturity is in their ability to truly listen to others' ideas without any reaction, especially when the opinions conflict with their own. Ideally there should be no need to become emotionally involved or confrontational when we are presented with arguments that differ from our religious, political, or lifestyle beliefs.

Savvy communicators know they don't have to attend every argument they are invited to, realizing conflicts can't survive without their participation. The wise can agree to disagree, thereby creating and maintaining lasting friendships by doing so.

It's been my experience that when our real friends reach out to us; want someone who can truly LISTEN with empathy, and no judgments. These true friends will have the BALLS to tell us things we may not want to hear, yet they will do it kindly with no intention to hurt us. We all have so-called friends who will never tell us what they think; for innumerable reasons stemming from not wanting to hurt your feelings or be dragged into a conflict especially when they know the other party you may be having difficulties with. I would humbly suggest that they may not be as intimate friends as we believe, but that's OK… we all have relationships of varying depths.

Your Legacy

Current news stories or fads are rarely remembered for long. It is not the extent of your life that matters; it's what you did with your time and how many lives you affected in positive ways. The measure of your life is not its duration but its donation. It's your life's width and depth, and how you treated people that will be considered.

Remember who you helped and were helped by. Our looks fade. What's important is the good we did while we were here. Our legacy is our testament to humanity.

The True Meaning of Becoming Liberal

Sadly, it seems to me that the word "Liberal" has become highly bemoaned in some circles. It's been chastised, politicized, and ostracized by many on the Far Right. For them, it's now synonymous with "Weakness." If one looks deeply into history, some of the greatest minds and teachers have chosen this path. Many ancient cultures as well have practiced charitable daily living and care for their fellow man and the environment. I see and feel what their statements, lifestyles, and teachings have produced in things today that were once criticized at the time of their initial inception. Their moral ideals are cherished and deeply valued by heart-centered and rationally thinking people globally.

323

It's hard for me to understand how mercy, charity, and compassion have been radicalized and poo-pooed by so many. It seems to me that avarice has replaced common sense and decency in regard to corporate boardrooms and operating mantras worldwide.

I shake my head and ask myself: "How much is enough and at what price must profit come?" I'm proud to be a Liberal – one who demonstrates compassion, gratitude, and random acts of kindness daily.

I see a Liberal as one who loves their fellow man; their planet, the dwindling world animal populations, disappearing natural resources and ecosystems. One doesn't need to be religious to engender or practice these qualities.

Forgiveness

When we carry the burden of non-forgiveness, we are the ones that suffer. As previously mentioned, forgiveness doesn't mean forgetting the past. We forgive others not because they deserve it, rather because we deserve peace. By doing so, we release a heavy burden. It takes a stronger person to do so. It's not easy. This doesn't mean we have to be around folks who caused us pain. I acknowledge what happened and try to remember their good points; after all, I did enjoy a better relationship with them at one time. I don't hate them; I simply choose not to have them in my life.

Self-Talk

Your self-talk has a dramatic impact on every aspect of your life. Lighten up on yourself and you'll gain a happier, more satisfying daily existence. Every living cell in your body has intelligence. Billions of them are listening 24/7 to everything you tell them. This is done with your words or the pictures your mind creates. They believe implicitly whatever you tell yourself. A little self-love goes a long way towards your inner peace.

Using Generosity as your Moral Compass

Generosity allows happiness to flow. Generous is an adjective described as liberal in giving or sharing; unselfish. Also, free from meanness, the smallness of mind or character; magnanimous. This speaks not only of giving physical items but the gift of one's time, perhaps in listening to another's problems without interruption or judgment.

This refers not only to what we give to others but also to ourselves. One need not be rich to share their wealth. No matter your current circumstances, we all have the same 24-hours in our days. Intelligent folks use their hours wisely.

Thomas E. Ziemann

Feed Your Soul

By recharging our bodies, mentally, physically, and emotionally, we nurture our inner wellbeing. In a sense, we are feeding our core being aka our connection to our soul. This begins by finding ones' "Positive Attitude Enhancers" By doing those things we find gratifying, heartfelt, or beneficial, we connect the circuit if you will. Here are a few ideas to do so.

Meditation

Herbal Supplements

Exercise

Nature

Time outs; clearing your head

Singing/Dancing

Therapy

Massage

Pets

Artistic Endeavors

Volunteering

Music, Listening/Playing

Long Drives

Sex

Sleep

Fishing

Motorcycle riding/Horse Back Riding

High adrenaline activities if that's your jam.

These are but a few things I came up with. You know what floats your boat. Do them and set yourself free.

Be Ready for Your Grand Awakening

I am convinced we were put on this planet to do more than merely exist, pay taxes, go to work at unfulfilling jobs and then come home, eat junky high-fat foods while plopping down in front of the boob-tube watching mindless comedies. Sadly, big business and governments would have you believe this. This sedentary lifestyle belongs to the scarcity mindset. This is your time to break out of this mold of mediocrity and move into Abundance Consciousness. Believing you are worthy to receive the good things life has to offer opens the door to cosmic connections.

My astute friend Tom Civiletti posed this question: "Consider how social manipulation through media could push people from abundance consciousness toward scarcity mindset. Consider why they might try that and why we should resist it?" Great points to ponder indeed. Time has come for a Grand

Awakening. Humans are becoming awake at an accelerated pace.

The questions to ask are:

Am I ready for it? How will my awareness be changed?

Remember that the Light at the end of the Tunnel in not the illusion, the Tunnel is." ~ Old Zen saying

Can I handle the Truth?

Much wisdom lies herein. This question resonates deep within my bones. To me this speaks of sharing; how to help people connect with their inner light. A worthy goal that can change the planet. This isn't some New Age, Pollyanna, pie in the sky, woo-woo statement. It is happening now. It is being witnessed and felt worldwide. History has already felt what merely a handful of Fully Awakened beings have done in the short periods they were sharing their wisdom.

Teachers like Yogananda, Jesus, Buddha, Vivekananda, Gandhi, Rumi, Krishna, Lao-Tzu, Mother Mary, Patanjali, Osho, The Dalai Lama, Eckhart Tolle, and Thich Nhat Hahn to mention but a few, have brought messages of hope to a darkened world.

For the best results, one's intentions must be aligned and accompanied by effort. This can be accomplished through congruence and "walking your talk."

The Most Important Question You Could Ever Ask Yourself

If you could choose only one single idea to focus on, it ought to be this one: "What specifically brings you real happiness?" Not temporary cheerfulness. Not a shopping trip to the mall. What is your single greatest source of joy? If you can answer this truthfully, I can tell you, gravitating towards that daily will help tremendously quell those inner demons you've been trying to rid yourself of. If you're not sure what your joy triggers are, take heart, since very few know exactly what makes them happy either.

One way to figure it out is knowing your joy triggers; those special things that evoke joy and make you happy! There is at least one that makes your soul sing. Making time for that one area of your life daily can transform your life.

Creating Gateways to Your Spiritual Core Being

It took me years to figure out that my religion was kindness. How you treat people you don't have to be nice to defines you. While anyone can claim to have or not have a religion, putting semantics aside, I believe the way one lives their life and treats others, including all creatures, is their religion. No church, temple, mosque, or synagogue is needed. Rather, acting with compassion, love, and kindness is all that's required.

We've all felt kindness' healing caress. It costs nothing yet returns so much to both the giver and receiver. Your small gestures can mean the world to someone who's dealing with painful inner demons that life sometimes manifests.

Try it and see how you feel as the direct result of sharing your inner light.

Do you know the difference between Happiness and Joy?

Great question indeed.

Happiness is an emotion in which one experiences feelings ranging from contentment and satisfaction to bliss and intense pleasure. Joy is much stronger! It's a much less common feeling than happiness; it's caused by elation at a moment in time.

Joy is derived from soul-satisfying, emotional wellbeing. Therefore, it's a deeper feeling of great pleasure and happiness. Joy may not always be about oneself but be about others' contentment.

Create your Life List-

I love this exercise! I found it somewhere online and felt immediately better after I filled in the blanks. No wrong answers, just your own.

Your Greatest Joy

_____

Your Greatest Feeling

_____

Your Greatest Problem to overcome

_____

Your Greatest Destructive Habit

_____

Your Greatest Loss

_____

Your Greatest Natural Resource

_____

Your Greatest Shot in the Arm

_____

Your Greatest Sleeping Pill

_____

Your Greatest Self Crippler

_____

Your Greatest Force in Life

_____

Your Greatest Asset

_____

Your Greatest Accomplishment

_____

Thomas E. Ziemann

Your Greatest Inner Feeling

___

Your Greatest Gift to People

___

Your Greatest Mantra

___

Your Greatest Leadership Quality

___

Your Greatest Motivator

___

Your Greatest Strength

___

Your Greatest Insight

___

Your Greatest Thing One Leaves Behind

___

Your Greatest Healing Force

___

Your Greatest Love In Your Life

___

Your Greatest Joy

___

Your Greatest Medication

___

Your Greatest Revitalizer

Your Greatest Unconditional Appreciation

Your Greatest Heart Kindler

Your Greatest Virtue

Your Ugliest Personality Traits

Creator Unknown

It Begins Within

Are you seeking the most incredible, loving relationship with someone? Perhaps you haven't met them yet or the initial spark seems to have dwindled in your current one. It all "Begins Within"!! By becoming our own best friend, we engender that long desired, nurturing feeling we've been pining for. Unless one accepts themselves "Completely, Fully and Unconditionally" it's unlikely they will attract, develop, or enjoy the grandiose fruits of what a fulfilling relationship can bestow upon them and the other.

I'm not speaking of narcissism here; simply openly and honestly accepting yourself wholly, your gifts, shortcomings, and those personal demons you haven't dealt with yet. By doing so, you can unlock those universal loving flood gates in which self-love can open.

One's self-talk has dramatic, impactful effects on every aspect of our lives. Lighten up on yourself; you'll experience a happier, more satisfying daily existence.

I have no Religion; my Religion is Kindness; right along with the Dalai Lama as he is fond of saying.

I am of the school of thought that how you treat people you don't have to be nice to, defines you. While anyone can claim to have or not have a religion, putting semantics aside, as stated ad nauseam in this book, the way one lives their life and treats others, including all creatures, is their religion. Acting with compassion, love, and kindness is all that's required.

When people have asked me what religion I practice, I simply say that I am on the path of Spirituality. They ask, what does that mean? For me, Spiritualty offers the richly rewarding gifts of self-discovery, connecting with one's core being and finding a higher purpose in their lives as a result. Moreover, I believe that evolved people take the spiritual world VERY seriously, like me they believe and feel there's much more to life than the physical dimension on which we currently exist.

It takes dedication and persistence combined with an open mind and heart; layered with compassion and forgiveness to walk the path of discernment. Something I have a long way to go on obtaining.

The Dalai Lama and Gandhi mastered Discernment.

No one can tell you what's right for you, nor should they, only they can determine that for themselves. The goal is not to believe anything you see, it's to challenge EVERYTHING!! Thereby one gleans greater wisdom and self-knowledge. Whether we agree or disagree with something is nowhere near as valuable as knowing why we believe as we do.

I've never liked the term "God" as I feel my understanding of God is well beyond my full comprehension. I find myself becoming anxious when someone tries to tell me how I should believe. Do I believe in a Universal mind? Zero doubt. In *The Department of Zenitation,*; I wrote that God is referred to as Elohim, El Shaddai, Our Heavenly Father, Lord, Yahweh, Jehovah, Jesus, Mohammed, Allah, and many other names. In Hinduism, Krishna is a popular name, although they have over 100 different names for God as well. In Pantheism, God is the universe itself.

Atheists may deny any kind of creator. Some physicists refer to God as a quantum field. Buddha's teachings resonate heavily with this perspective. Although he didn't use the same vernacular, he did teach that everything is connected. The point here is that since the dawn of humanity, all races of people have had some inclination for understanding spirit.

My purpose is not to try to convince anyone of anything. We all have our thoughts of what makes our reality. Moreover, the idea of God is far too vast for a tiny chapter, That said, allow me to share a few of my thoughts and beliefs.

The best explanation of GOD I have ever read goes:

God Is Conscious, not a creator. God is the Source of creation itself. IT, (not he or she) IT is not independent of you. IT's the totality of everything. So when I call myself God, I am not talking about myself. I am talking about the expression of the God-self that rests inside of me. The verb, the energy…not the noun. Once you think of God as a noun, person, place, or thing, you separate yourself from it and immediately become a limited being. That's what separates the believers (religion) from the knowers (spiritual).

This gave me a starting point of reference to take as my own.

I love that the premise that God is simply a metaphor for the Universe; we are all made in its image. Check out the staggering number of scientific photos of brain cells compared to the universe, the birth of cells compared to the death of stars, and the uncanny likeness between them. Their unmistakable similarity is amazing, to say the least.

No matter what religion or path one chooses there is something within each of us that, without any suggestion, urges us to make the correct choice or do the right thing. If you listen, you can hear it loudly, not in words. I'm not sure that Source speaks like that, but it appears more like a deep heartfelt sensation.

For this reason, I believe all humans are basically good and usually make the best choices they can within the limits of their awareness at the time of action.

It's been said there's a golden thread of truth that runs through all religions. My first guru used to say: "Religions all tell the truth and yet they all lie."

God has no place of worship but the soul. Source cannot be approached through a false self-image. It's been said that every religion borrows from other forms that preceded them. I have many friends who have stated they don't have any particular religion. They claim that they try to do the right thing when no one is looking and to be true to themselves.

I reply: "That's wonderful. Then your religion is one of Spirituality. One that requires no name, but simply to be and always attempting to be one's best self and to have a true love for oneself."

These friends of mine I speak of are deep thinkers. Since thinking is a spiritual practice, I remind them to take time daily to think of deep matters, as well to take time "not to think, "just to exist in the eternal now, to focus on their breath and give gratitude. No specific place is required; any place can be one's temple. However, I find it quite refreshing to be out in the forest, basking at a lake, sitting by the ocean, hanging in the desert or being high atop a mountain. Just about any place in nature can help one feel closer to Source, even one's backyard.

Quantum physics is related to the reason there are so many different religions. When physicists look at data, some see waves, and some see particles. Both see what they want, which is perfect. Quantum mechanics refers to them as wave-particle; an entity that simultaneously has the properties of a wave and a particle, i.e. "Waveicals." My theory states that God is pure vibration, this force exists everywhere, and the particles are different aspects of this vibration, a.k.a. other religions. I've always believed God was too large for one religion anyway. Perhaps the Higgs-Boson particle will someday give up more clues in the collider.

A particularly good friend of mine, Dr. Steve McSwain posted the following questions on his Facebook page a few years ago. I've added my responses below to his questions.

He posted: "Which of the following statements are true? It takes spiritual practice to reach the presence of God. God, Spirit, Universal Consciousness, Vibration, The Primordial OM, whatever term one prefers is always present. It takes no practice to reach it. It is always omnipresent.

That said, if one wants a deeper connection, the seeker will need to figure out which method(s) work best for them. Prayer, meditation, as well as spending time in nature, are among the hundreds of ways to get closer to Source. One need not be religious to do so. Atheists can connect with it.

Again, the key is daily practice. Are you being in the Presence already, and nothing to Reach?"

100% agreement. The question that needs pondering is:

What kind of relationship does one aspire to?

Are you being the Presence of God yourself?

100% agreement. There is a golden shard, a sliver, a piece of the Divine existing within all things. What one is seeking, is also seeking them. Everything is connected.

In Vedic tradition, they would speak of this connection as Indra's Net of Jewels. In Christianity, "We are like unto him" Exodus 15:11. Hindus believe the Divine resides in all beings.

By accepting the divinity in all beings and all of nature, Hinduism views the universe as a family, in Sanskrit, Vasudhaiva Kutumbakam; All beings, from the smallest organism to man, are considered manifestations of God.

I will leave this chapter with the following story. A Father wanted to connect on a deeper level with his Son who was becoming a young man. So, he planned a few Father/Son getaways...just the two of them. The first Saturday the Father took his Son to the forest. It was a beautiful summer day. The dappled sunlight shone brightly amidst the treetops lining the well-traveled footpath below them. The smells emanating from the trees were exquisite.

They sat down under a large Douglas fir to enjoy their lunch. The Son mentioned to his Father. OK, we are here, so where is the forest? The Father was silent for a second, he grinned widely and said Son, "you" are the Forest. They both remained quiet and enjoyed their picnic while a slight breeze was blowing. The following week the Father planned another outing, this time to the Oregon coast. They parked the car and meandered down the sandy, seaweed-riddled walkway.

The golden sun had broken through the cotton-like, billowing clouds just as a gray whale breached the foamy waves offshore, a spectacular sight to behold. They walked a while taking in the majestic serene scenery. The Newport salty ocean spray caressed their windswept, sunlit faces. Seagulls cawed breaking up the calm momentarily. The Son posed another question to his Father; Dad, I love the beach, but where is the Ocean? Without hesitation, his father smiled and said, Son, "you" are the ocean.

This time the Son snapped back, "How could you give me the same answer you did the last time when we were in the forest?" The Father paused and said, "Great question. I believe that there is a loving vibration, a golden thread if you will, that connects all things. I have felt its warm presence for many years. There are many names for this Source, which matter not. I believe that there is no religion in the spirit world.

What does matter is to realize that we are connected to all things, living or inanimate. We, therefore, are all that we see and do not. The son pondered what his father shared and said: "Where is this source?" "It exists everywhere on every level," his father replied. "How can I find it?" the son asked with a glimmer in his eye. His Father smiled once again, "When you see the beautiful shoreline, how does it make you feel?" The Son thought for a moment and replied, "It's awesome, I like how I feel when I'm near it, see it or even think of it." The Father said, "That's good, that's the vibration I am speaking of, you already knew of it whether you put a name on it."

The Son quickly remarked; "How can I understand this vibration thing better?" Without hesitation, the Father replied, "It exists within all of us. One way to experience it is to focus on that silent place in your mind. Place no judgments or expectations of what you will experience. Simply allow yourself to connect with it. Sit quietly; focus on your breath is all that's required."

The two were silent, both enjoying the deeper bond they had created.

How do you define Spirit?

What brings you peace?

How do you live it on a daily basis?

PART TWO:

TRANSFORM THE QUALITY OF YOUR RELATIONSHIPS

Relationship Coach Jennifer Blankl offers her
insights to help you feel relationship ready.

CHAPTER 30:

THE REAL REASON YOU EITHER FEEL STUCK OR FULFILLED IN RELATIONSHIPS

Why do you at times feel joyful, fulfilled, or even and euphoric, while other times you feel emotionally stuck (I call it being in a "funk") where you don't want to feel the way you do, but you do? You stay there. Like when you stay mad at your partner when they've triggered you, even when you wish the argument could be resolved and done with.

What's really driving your deepest feelings, thoughts and choices in life and in your relationships? What's your real motivation in everything you are feeling and doing? Why do you resist that deeper conversation with a loved one, that feels riskier, but could build deeper understanding and compassion? Why does your partner retreat in to his "man cave" after work and play video games instead of connecting with you?

Why do you stay on Facebook an extra 30 minutes while your partner nags you to get off ?

THE ANSWER: TO MEET ONE OR MORE OF YOUR HUMAN NEEDS!!

Feelings and emotions arise when our need are met or not met, which happens at every moment of life. By connecting our feelings with our human needs, we can take full responsibility for our thoughts, feelings and choices, freeing us and others from fault and blame.

Because at the end of the day, we all have a good intention, to meet our human needs. And that good intention remains whether we use high-level (good for us long term) or low-level (not good for us long-term) strategies to get them met. After all, we are human. And we are wired to act and feel in ways that ultimately give us a sense that our needs are being met.

Now what I'm about to teach you is the very tool that transformed my own Marriage and my life. When my husband lost an 11-year job through no fault of his own when I was pregnant with our first son, I had no idea what was happening to him as a man, because I didn't understand his needs, nor my own. So I blamed him. I blamed him for the way he was showing up for me, the way I felt he wasn't treating me right or connecting with me the way I needed.

I failed to understand how his most valued needs were attached to his significance, success and certainty at work, while my most valued needs revolve around growth and love and connection.

Becoming an expert in the 6 Human Needs transformed me and the way I show up for my husband, the way I think, feel and treat him. That in turn allowed him to be more of the man I needed and wanted, even through the immense pain and challenges he was facing at the time. I'm beyond grateful for having learned this tool and I teach it with determination and passion to my private individual and couple clients as well as in my workshops.

I invite to learn this powerful, life-changing strategy too, so you can make a long-term transformation in your own life and love relationship.

So here we go....

Human Needs Psychology research shows all humans share 6 Human Needs. These 6 needs are universal to humans since we share the same neurological system. What makes each of us unique, and what makes relationships require so much work, is the fact that we individually favor two needs over the other four. These top two needs are essentially your blueprint, your deepest driving force and motivation in everything you're feeling, thinking and doing. The strategies and vehicles we choose to meet our needs, especially the two we favor most, determine our fulfillment level in life.

The most powerful breakthrough in life comes when you discover what your own top two needs are, how you're going about getting them met, your "rules" for getting them met, because now, you can make much clearer sense of all that's happening in your world and in your most valued relationships.

Here are the 6 Universal Human Needs:

Love & Connection: the need to feel close and bonded to others; feeling

accepted, understood and included.

Significance: the need to feel needed, admired, respected, important, worthy, special.

Certainty: the need to feel like you can avoid pain and gain pleasure. Stability, predictability, security.

Uncertainty/Variety: the need for excitement; stimulation, the unpredictable side of life.

Growth: The need to expand ourselves mentally, spiritually, emotionally.

Contribution: The need to get out of our own head, go beyond our self and give back to others.

All day, every day we are making attempts (mainly subconsciously) to get one or more of these 6 Human Needs met. These attempts include the FEELINGS we feel, the THOUGHTS we think, and the CHOICES and ACTIONS we decide to take propel you in a whole new, much more fulfilling and joyful direction in your life and relationships!

TAKE ACTION. Take this test. Get a fresh new perspective on the deeper roots underneath your thoughts, emotions and actions. Make deeper sense of what's driving you. This human needs knowledge can make you go from frustrated, confused, and even feeling hopeless... to feeling empowered with a new wealth of knowledge about yourself and those you most love.

So, what are your top two needs?

What are your partner's top two needs?

What has to happen for you to feel like each of your top needs are being met?

What has to happen for your partner for them to feel like their top needs are being met?

Do these "rules" for what has to happen make it easier or harder for you, and your partner, to feel like your needs are being met at a higher level?

Begin here. Learn what your top needs are and get clear on how you go about meeting each of your needs specifically.

And let this new knowledge be the fuel that motivates you to be the one to transform your relationship and your life! I'd love to hear about your own "AHAs" and breakthroughs after discovering your own top two needs and assessing how your daily reality reflects your own awesome Needs blueprint. Let me answer your questions. Feel free to email me anytime at jen@jenniferblankl.com with your questions for a personal response from me!

If you're ready and wanting to transform your own relationship, I invite you to apply for a FREE 30-minute private coaching consult with me to address your own personal dynamic or challenge and how that relates to your human needs. Together, we'll solidify a strategy that you can act on to start an immediate shift.

These are bonuses for readers of this book. **http://www.jenniferblankl.com/**

1. Seven Powerful Exercises to Instantly Connect with your Love Partner:

http://www.jenniferblankl.com/7-powerful-exercises/

2. Discover Your Top 2 Needs (the six universal human needs test):

http://www.jenniferblankl.com/what-are-your-top-2-needs/

3. Your Ultimate Relationship Vision Exercise:

http://www.jenniferblankl.com/relationship-vision/

It only takes one person to transform a relationship, and that person is YOU!

CHAPTER 31:

RELATIONSHIP WITH SELF/SELF-CARE

Do you give yourself full permission to put yourself first guilt free and still feel like the Rockstar professional/parent/partner you truly are? I hear people often-times say, "My relationship hasn't been my biggest priority, caring for myself is hard enough!!" The truth is, when we fail at taking care of ourselves, we can't take care of and serve anyone else as much as we really want. Heck, we don't even FEEL like it because feeling stretched thin and operating in burnout mode has hijacked our emotional state. When we abandon our own self-care, we sacrifice the energy, the mindset, the confidence, the belief systems, and the emotional state that we need to show up in this life at our highest level for both ourselves and for those we love.

You must put your well-being and self first. You're not doing anyone else any favors otherwise. I'll say it again - you're not helping anyone else by sacrificing your own self-care. Self-care is not selfish. It's about being able to give of yourself at your highest level. The world benefits far greater from a well-cared-for you.

Recently, a male client expressed how much he appreciated the fact that his girlfriend took action to get the professional help she needed to break through her "emotional flatness", as he called it. Prior to her getting help, he had expressed a lot of pain, frustration and upset around her non-action and inability to crawl out of the rut she was in. As her partner, he felt helpless,

because he couldn't seem to assist her, while at the same time, feeling disconnected from her and unable to get her help in meeting his own needs. So when she made the conscious effort and decision to get her own help, which led to her shift, his first feeling and response was appreciation. Because for him, her loving herself enough to get the help she needed to shift, was in essence, loving him better.

Emotional State Mastery

WE 'DO' OUR EMOTIONS.

Although it often doesn't feel like it our emotions are not simply happening TO us, we choose them. We engage with them. We expand them and 'do 'them by choice. We tend to make this decision subconsciously, but when we can get aware, we can choose to do another emotion at any time.

We all know a person that is easily angered or the person that tends to go inward and feel more sadness and depression when things aren't right in their world. Interestingly, we 'do' our emotions because they meet one or more of our needs. Even the emotions that keep us stuck and feeling rotten, have power over us because they're meeting one or more underlying needs. Because of this, we can slip into emotional patterns and habits without even realizing we're doing so, leaving us wondering why we feel so stuck in a life dilemma or in a relationship challenge.

For example, think of a time you were mad at your partner, so mad that you held on to your anger a while withholding your love and compassion for them because you really wanted them to 'pay' for the pain you're feeling from that thing they said or did. Remember how much your argument hurt yet you remained entrenched in it. You stayed in the fight, and even added fuel to the fire. So why do we stay stuck in these painful dynamics? What prevents us from wising up, taking a pause, and climbing out of our ruts? The reason is that our emotions, even the super shitty ones, meet our needs. That's right. They meet our human needs - the needs we must meet every day to survive.

The trick is, we can meet them at high levels, in ways that fulfill us, or we can humanly meet them at low levels, using forms and ways that don't fulfill us or make us feel good in the long run. These are "false rewards" that feel good for the short term but can sabotage our long term. When we fight unproductively with our partner, we inadvertently get some of our human needs met, although at a lower level that doesn't fulfill us in the long run, but still we get them met. For example, arguing can give us a feeling of power because we're withholding from our partner in effort to punish them; we're competing; and defending. In this case, you could get your need for significance met- your universal human need to feel important, respected, valued, needed, and enough. We can also meet our universal human need for love and connection in our worst arguments, for now we (finally) have our partner's full and undivided attention.

For many couples who don't get to see their partners or connect with them meaningfully as often as they need, arguing and engaging in conflict can fill the gaps created by a lack of attention, and/or quality time together. We can also meet our universal human need for certainty and comfort by avoiding having to address the deeper root cause of relationship pain, which can feel most uncertain, and most uncomfortable.

FORGIVENESS

Forgiving another person is for ourselves, not the other person. When we forgive, we free ourselves from the toxic, burdening emotions that come with holding on to resentment, anger, contempt, etc. Choosing not to forgive is much more a form of self-punishment than making the other person pay. The interesting thing is, holding someone hostage through staying angry with them, can give us a sense of power, certainty, and control, perhaps a distraction from an even bigger problem. The ways anger and withdrawal of love can help us feel like we're getting our needs met is the driving motivation oftentimes for us to stay stuck.

"Unforgiveness is drinking the poison and waiting for your enemy to die." ~ Nelson Mandela

GIVE YOURSELF PERMISSION TO STOP BEING ANGRY!

Are you finding it hard to forgive your partner?

Oprah Winfrey has said "Forgiveness is giving up the hope that the past could have been any different than it actually was."

Forgiveness is for you and different then "making amends" with someone.

In what ways could you be unconsciously holding on to unforgiveness in an attempt to make someone pay?

Where is this showing up in your relationship and in your life lately? What impact does this have on you and your relationship? What are the costs of unforgiveness? What does it cost you emotionally? How much precious time do you spend on unforgiveness?

What experiences do you sacrifice through unforgiveness? How else does it cost you, specifically? How do you feel about the above definition of forgiveness and unforgiveness now?

What could you gain by forgiving someone in your life you have yet to forgive, and freeing yourself? What could you feel? What could you now experience? What can you now do? Who can you now be?

CHAPTER 32:

ELEVATION STRATEGY: LOOKING FOR THE HIGHER INTENT IN YOUR OWN AND OTHER PEOPLE'S BEHAVIOR

Using this strategy will help you elevate any relationship.

Ever wonder why a loved one acts or behaves the way they do, even when directed toward you? Perhaps their behavior causes you hurt and pain. Maybe you feel stuck as far as why they act the way they do. It feels personal.

What gives?

What if, in these more challenging relationship moments, we were able to elevate the other person by seeing a higher intention in their behavior.

Don't think they could possibly have a "good intention" here? What if I told you everything we do (our thoughts, focus, actions and decisions) are all driven by the needs we value most. We've all got a higher intention, believe it or not, in all of our functional and dysfunctional behavior and that's to get a need, or needs, met. We're often not aware of this, for we do it mostly subconsciously - meeting our needs that is.

What if the new question became:

What needs are you/they trying to meet through their actions and behavior? When you ask this question instead, you elevate your thinking, you elevate your mind and you elevate the other person. In turn, you elevate your relationship.

You can choose the meaning you will attach to another's behavior and choices. And when we come from a place of choice, we typically show up better for others in our lives by becoming more empathetic and compassionate about exactly where they are at instead of relying on our own filters and unconscious judgments. Don't assume you know why someone is doing what they're doing! We need to get more curious about our love partners and the key people in our lives.

There are so many gifts to be had by being more generous with other people's intentions.

It takes very little effort or awareness to judge or assess someone else's behavior and choices but when we get better about seeing our deeds and other people's actions through the lenses of the 6 Universal Human Needs, we get better about seeing the higher intention our own and others' actions and can get much better at having meaningful, intentional and deeply fulfilling relationships. Our human needs drive all of our functional and dysfunctional behavior.

CHAPTER 33:

WHY LOVE IS ALWAYS WORTH THE RISK AND PAIN

Very dear friends from Southern California just visited us for four days. This is a girlfriend of mine I've had for a couple of decades now, her incredible husband and brilliant son. This friend knows my deepest darkest secrets. She has seen me at both my best and my worst, and she still loves me and shows up as my true and loyal friend year after year. We had an absolutely incredible time during their stay with us.

My two boys bonded especially more so than ever with their son this visit. The trio of them were like three peas in a pod the entire trip, having fun, with unusually little bickering for boys. The seven of us laughed together, teared up together, shared stories and updates, escaped auto-pilot mode and work routine together, told inappropriate jokes and shared extremely personal stories, ate like kings, and had our fair share of beverages. Together.

An hour ago, we stood on the driveway, gave our second round of hugs to the three of them, blew kisses and waved goodbye. My boys chased them down the street like little puppies as they drove away. And as I turned around to go back inside the house, it hit me like a ton of bricks. OUCH. THEY'RE GONE. THEY LEFT. And then the tears began to flood my eyes and I got that puzzled look I get from the boys when I go from smiling to crying in half a second. And then my 7-year-old begins to cry and says, "I miss Josh! We didn't even get to see him for long!" We went inside and sat on the stairs together and just let ourselves cry for a bit. Then I looked at him and I said, "You know why we feel this sadness right now? It's because we are SO, SO fortunate to be able to experience the love and connection (1 of the 6 Universal Human Needs), the euphoria and nostalgia, the funny and memorable conversations and meaningful exchanges with such good and true friends... that we feel the emotional pain and loss when they leave. So in essence, our sadness is a gift, because it allows us to feel how important and sacred certain people are to us in our life. We wouldn't feel such "loss" if they weren't so significant to us." My son lifted up his little head and wiped the tears from his eyes and said. "Yeah, I know, Mommy."

So after some more time I started thinking, that this is one of the dilemmas of romantic love and relationships! The more attached we get to another person, the more "pain" we may perceive we are at risk of experiencing from the relationship. The way we perceive that risk both consciously and subconsciously, directly determines how close or attached we will allow ourselves to become to other people throughout our entire life.

Now I know my above personal example is a much easier emotional pain to experience and get over because it's a positive one. I know I'll see our good friends again. But my point here is to highlight the greater gifts and joy and excitement we get to experience from spending quality time with those we love and giving them our full presence, by being there for them, by investing our time, energy and emotions in them, and all of the life and love fuel we get from nurturing our key relationships so far outweighs any potential pain and/or loss we may experience.

CHAPTER 34:

OUR LOVE LANGUAGES

Do you ever feel frustrated with your efforts to connect and show love and appreciation for your partner only to be met NOT with the reaction you were wanting and expecting? Just the other day a client was complaining about how exhausted she is from upping her compliments and appreciation game with her husband, only to be met with a lackadaisical response. She felt extremely frustrated and rejected in her attempt to give him love in this form. However, his preference is solidly 'quality time'. He misses her, as she comes home late from running the business every day. He craves her next to him, her attention and presence, that her complimentary words aren't able to make the cut because his top love language is far from being tended to, even though she's putting in tons of effort. Just not the RIGHT effort that aligned with his preferred way of receiving her love. In other words, she was loving him in the

wrong love language. She thought she was on track because she was loving him in the way she wanted to be.

5 LOVE LANGUAGES:

Do you ever feel unappreciated for your, effort, time and sacrifice you make for your Love Partner? Ever feel like no matter what you do or how much you give to your Partner to make them happy, it doesn't get you the result you're after in your relationship. How do YOU most love to receive love? What about your partner? How does he or she love to receive love most?

How do you love to be loved the most? Is it through kind and affirming words being spoken to you? Is it someone giving you their undivided attention and full presence? Is it through physical touch? Or receiving a gift from someone? Or is it when someone does something for you through acts of service?

Knowing what your "Love Language" is (Thank you Dr. Gary Chapman!) is a complete GAME CHANGER in your personal and romantic relationships! Our natural human tendency is to love our partner and others in the way WE, OURSELVES prefer to receive love. It took me too long to realize just because my preferred love language is 'words of affirmation,' doesn't mean my husband must appreciate compliments and verbal praise the way I do. As a matter of fact, verbal compliments and affirmations don't mean much to him, because his love language is 'acts of service'.

Things I DO are what makes him feel most loved. And even though this attempt can come with the best of intentions, giving love to others in the form that we prefer versus what THEY prefer leads to so much unnecessary misunderstanding and disappointment, rejection and hurt feelings, not to mention exhaustion from all the wasted energy and effort. Get clear on your own preferred love language and those you love. It can really help you gain so much more insight into how you, and others you love, prefer to be loved.

ACKNOWLEDGEMENTS

In any project, there are a myriad of steps that must be accomplished to bring it to its fruition. In this book, for example, there are so many people to applaud and thank. Forgive me if I missed anyone.

Huge thanks to **Dr. Christian Conte**, your wisdom and kindness are beyond reproach. **Dr. Bernie Siegel** for always being willing to help other people.

My editor Edie Weinstein, your velvet pen never ceases to amaze.

Co-Contributor: **Jennifer Blankl**, for your contributions to this collaboration.

Creative Consultants: **Lisa Peplow, Dorothy Cramer, and Austin Vickers**; each of your helpful ideas and suggestions helped improve this book. **Eric Labacz**, your covers, and interior designs are brilliant! Heartfelt thanks to all the professionals who endorsed this book by name. All of the reviewers who added their pithy prose. Everyone in our focus groups who shared their ideas, as well as the plethora of online sources that were used when researching this book.

Big shout out to my longtime friend, **Noho Marchesi** for your support, generosity, and huge Hawaiian heart, my brother. Master "Ho", has touched literally thousands of lives.

Lastly, to my beautiful wife **Michelle**. You have helped me grow emotionally and spiritually with your patience and forgiving nature. My occasional rampant ego replete with overwhelming childlike enthusiasm has driven some people crazy. Thank you for accepting me, my flaws, and loving me as you do.

I love you all.

Your relationship has ended. Before jumping blindly
into the next one, consider the following before
moving on.

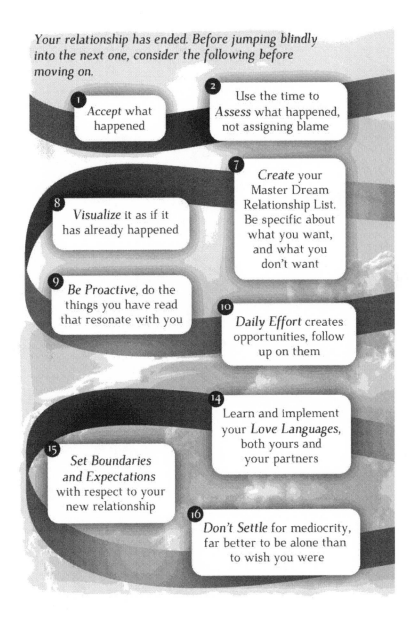

1 *Accept* what happened

2 Use the time to *Assess* what happened, not assigning blame

7 *Create* your Master Dream Relationship List. Be specific about what you want, and what you don't want

8 *Visualize* it as if it has already happened

9 *Be Proactive*, do the things you have read that resonate with you

10 *Daily Effort* creates opportunities, follow up on them

14 Learn and implement your *Love Languages*, both yours and your partners

15 *Set Boundaries and Expectations* with respect to your new relationship

16 *Don't Settle* for mediocrity, far better to be alone than to wish you were

3 Take appropriate time to *Grieve*

4 *Address* any issues that you need to work on as you start to heal past wounds

6 Give yourself the *Love* you deserve, treating yourself as you would want a partner to treat you

5 *Forgive* yourself and your ex, thereby giving yourself inner peace

11 When you find a potential good match, set the *Groundwork* for success

12 Use effective, direct *Communication* with your new relationship. Make sure you both know each other's wants, needs, desires and expectations

13 Don't confuse *Love with Lust*; give your new relationship time to know the difference

18 *Don't rush it*, dream relationships take time to build. There is no set timeline to achieve a happy, healthy relationship

17 Stay Positive, open to Possibilities and do the work required

Manufactured by Amazon.ca
Bolton, ON